Advance Praise for

The Maker Versus the Takers

"We can no more stop participating in economics than we can suspend breathing, drinking water, or eating. That makes economics as spiritual as any other dimension of our existence, and Jesus had a lot to say about it. You won't find a better guide to what Jesus said about economics than *The Maker Versus the Takers*, and there's never been a better time to consider the topic than right now!"

—Joseph Castleberry, Ed.D., president, Northwest University
and author of *The Kingdom Net: Learning to Network Like Jesus*

"Jesus is too often misunderstood. Biblical Christianity can be seen as irrelevant when we fail to both understand the historical context and use it for a better lens for contemporary application. Jerry Bowyer offers a provocative and critical set of insights into how economics and geopolitical factors shaped the Gospel narratives in a way that helps us consider how Jesus would have us engage our present world as ambassadors of the Jesus Administration. Stimulating, beneficial, and disturbing in a good way!"

—Mike Sharrow, CEO, The C12 Group

"Jerry Bowyer takes on the sensitive question of 'can wealth be righteous?' Curiously, this was a political question even in the days of Jesus. If you have ever wondered what Jesus thought of wealth or why the rich young ruler was turned away, then *The Maker Versus the Takers* is for you."

—Gordon Robertson, president, The Christian
Broadcasting Network

THE
MAKER

VERSUS

THE
TAKERS

THE
MAKER
VERSUS
THE
TAKERS

WHAT JESUS REALLY SAID
ABOUT SOCIAL JUSTICE
AND ECONOMICS

JERRY BOWYER

FIDELIS
BOOKS

A FIDELIS BOOKS BOOK
An Imprint of Post Hill Press

The Maker Versus the Takers:
What Jesus Really Said About Social Justice and Economics
© 2020 by Jerry Bowyer
All Rights Reserved

ISBN: 978-1-63758-675-4
ISBN (eBook): 978-1-64293-371-0

Post Hill Press
New York • Nashville
posthillpress.com

Published in the United States of America

Everything I do, I do to glorify God,
to impress Susan and to make things better
for my children (and as of now) one grandchild.
This book is dedicated to the same.

CONTENTS

INTRODUCTION

This all started with a phone call to my radio show. A woman called in to attack me for not supporting socialism. "Jesus said that it's easier for a camel to go through the eye of a needle than for a rich man to go to heaven." The answer popped immediately to my mind: "But He said it about a senator, and you want to give senators like this even more money and power."

So, it started two decades ago with a debate, but over time I grew hungry to do more than just win the argument or to merely defend my views against shallow attempts to use the Bible to discredit them. I grew hungry to understand what Jesus really was saying, if He was saying anything at all, about economics.

This book is written for people who share that same hunger, who really want to know what Jesus said about economics. It may seem too obvious to mention, but in order to have a Christian view of economics, we need to study what Jesus said about it. Unfortunately, a great deal of the Christian commentary on economics is based on ideas that have been *brought to* the Gospel texts, rather than *drawn out* of them. I've been wrestling with these questions since I rejected Marx and embraced Jesus thirty-seven years ago. Since I was a Marxist before becoming a Christian, I gravitated toward reading books about Christianity and economics, particularly Christian refutations of Marx.

What I saw then is pretty much the same as I've seen since: people taking their best thinking and hanging it on a Scriptural passage. Folks on the left took their best thinking (which in my estimation then and now is not very good thinking) and hung it on some text from the Gospels or the prophets. They formulated a Marxian concept of justice and then simply read it into the text every time the word "justice" was used. You see, they first decided what was right and then concluded, since it was right, Jesus must have believed the same thing.

We free-market types had better economics but still tended to read our views into the text or, worse, attempted to shield ourselves from the text by spiritualizing away Jesus's references to the poor or to debt. Some of us push Jesus's economic message off to the distant future when He returns and the Kingdom comes.

Millennial Christians sensed a tension between Jesus's confrontations with wealthy people on the one hand and the attempts of free-market advocates to explain them away on the other. Many of these millennial Christians mistakenly embraced what they thought was a left-wing Jesus. They clustered around the movement that came to be called "red letter" Christianity, a name that refers to versions of the Bible that print Jesus's direct words in red ink. These progressives were saying to their conservative elders that they, unlike the conservatives, embraced Jesus's actual words, including clear denunciations of wealth.

And that's where we're stuck, between "red letter Christians" and Christians who understand the true dangers of centrally planned economies but shy away from quoting Jesus's tough talk about economic exploitation. This book will argue forcefully that Jesus's denunciations of the wealthy are not calls for government expansions—on the contrary, they are denunciations of those who wielded expanded state power.

This book is for those of you who want to become unstuck and maybe, by the grace of God, help the debate become unstuck.

To get the blessings of Jesus, we must really want to know what He taught and to follow Him wherever He leads. I have tried to do that with all of my heart, soul, mind, and strength through deep dives into original languages and groundbreaking (literal and figurative) findings in the economic archeology of ancient Galilee, and careful study of the historical context of the Gospels via near contemporaries of Jesus, such as Philo, Josephus, the rabbis who wrote the Mishnah, early church fathers, and pagans such as Tacitus. At every point I thought I saw something, I asked God to show me what You really mean here and give me the willingness to drop a theory of mine, no matter how exciting it was or how well it would preach, if the text did not back up that theory.

What emerged from that process amazed me with its clarity. But what struck me more powerfully was the way that, over and over, in hundreds of ways, the details of the Biblical texts exhibited the same pattern.

What the Gospel accounts showed was a Jesus who was very concerned about economic exploitation, but whose economic denunciations were not broad, to-whom-it-may-concern condemnations of all wealth. Instead, He directed His denunciations in very specific geographical and socioeconomic ways, aiming His barbs at the exploitative members of the ruling class.

A close and careful reading of the Gospels allows us to fully embrace and quote the "red letters" of a Jesus who said, "Woe unto you who are rich...," without going on to confuse Him with Che Guevara or Fidel Castro.

What you will see is Jesus confronting the takers of wealth, not the makers of it. He did this with such vigor and clarity, the ruling class who lived and worked in that nation's capital saw Him as a threat to their system of economic extraction. That's why they instigated His judicial execution by the Roman state. Elites failed to heed Jesus's warnings about the ways in which the capital city and its ruling political/religious elite were courting disaster. Eventually, the economic problems Jesus warned about led to an economic collapse and the destruction of the capital city, Jerusalem.

You are about to meet a Jesus who really does have something to say about social justice, but not the kind of social justice people have been selling in His name.

That's the theory. Now for the evidence.

PART I

How to See the Economics in the Gospels

To Understand Jesus's Economics, Stop Skimming Over the Geographical Details

I've spent decades sitting in pews listening to sermons and in Bible studies listening to Bible study leaders, and what I've noticed is what preachers and teachers tend not to notice—place names. Mostly when people read the Bible, they seem to skim over details like place names in order to get to "the main point." But when it comes to the Bible, it's all the main point:

> *All Scripture is inspired by God and profitable for teaching, for reproof, for correction, for training in righteousness; so that the man of God may be adequate, equipped for every good work.*
>
> —2 Timothy 3:16–17

That's "all Scripture," which means all the words in Scripture are literally God-breathed, and God does not waste His breath. Words like Nazareth, Galilee, Bethsaida, Caesarea Philippi, Capernaum, Bethany, Jerusalem, and Jericho are the words telling us where the events of the

Bible transpire, including and especially the events in the life of Jesus described in the Gospels.

Jesus was a traveling teacher, who, unlike the foxes and the birds, had no holes or nests in which to lay His head.

And Jesus said to him, "The foxes have holes, and the birds of the air have nests, but the Son of Man has nowhere to lay His head."

—LUKE 9:58

He lived "on the road," and the Gospels quite often tell us specifically to which cities and villages the road took Him. Have your teachers paid close attention to those place names? Have you? If we don't follow those details, then we are more likely to read our own economic views into the Gospels than to get our economic views from the Bible.

All the details in the Old Testament Torah were of eternal consequences, even individual letters...

For truly I say to you, until heaven and earth pass away, not the smallest letter or stroke shall pass from the Law until all is accomplished.

—MATTHEW 5:18

So, of course, place names in the New Testament are important too. Ancient publishing was a very expensive proposition. Both the medium (the ink and the page) and the labor (from highly skilled experts called scribes) were rare and costly. Space was not wasted—so much so that not until later, when publishing became cheaper, were spaces between words and punctuation added. The earliest copies we have of the Gospels (and they are very early indeed) had neither spaces nor punctuation. If publishing was so expensive and compressed that it didn't have room for a space or a period, can we really believe "Bethsaida" can be treated as an extraneous detail? No, the geographical markers are there for good reason.

If we don't know those reasons, we, and not the Bible, need to change if we are going to achieve a more accurate understanding of the Scriptures. This is especially true when Jesus is making observations about economics. Every time He says something about wealth, He is standing somewhere, and wherever people live, there is some kind of economic base. That economic base provides context in which to understand Jesus's words.

This is an automatic thing you do when you read accounts of events in your own time and place.

If you read a story that occurs in Silicon Valley and a young man in a T-shirt steps out of a mansion, you are very likely to have a preconceived notion about what industry he works in—information technology. A narrator would almost be obliged to inform you if he does not work in that field to make sure you do not misread the account.

I am writing this book where I live, in the Mon Valley area of Pittsburgh. If you were to watch a movie set here in the 1950s, you are likely to assume the characters work in heavy industry, probably in steel. The guy in the suit is probably an executive; the guy carrying a lunchbox works in the factory and is a union member.

You get the idea: New York—finance. Houston—oil. Hollywood—movies. Washington, DC—politics. Remember that last one on the list: DC. What we will see is Jesus's conversations about money take on a more and more adversarial tone the closer He gets to His version of DC: Jerusalem.

What about Bethlehem? Do you have associations with that? Of course you do. You think of it as the place where Jesus was born. But that's because you come after Jesus was born there, you've seen the Christmas pageants and the movies, and you've read the stories in the Gospels. But before Jesus was born there, it was not known as the birthplace of Jesus. It carried a different set of associations.

The first people who heard the nativity stories did not hear the word Bethlehem and think about Christmas pageants. Contemporaries would probably have thought about sheep since that was the local industry. The town was known for sheep. Any particular kind of sheep? Yes, Bethlehem was where they bred lambs for export to Jerusalem to be used in temple sacrifices.

That's right, Jesus was the Lamb of God, who bears away the sins of the world, and He was born in the one city named by the rabbis as the place designated for the breeding of sacrificial lambs.

Alfred Edersheim was a leading Hebrew scholar who converted to Christianity, but not before thoroughly mastering the Hebrew Scriptures and rabbinic commentary (to the degree those things can be mastered by any mere mortal). In his important book, *The Life and Times of Jesus the Messiah*, he talked about Bethlehem as discussed in the Mishnah (the rabbinical commentary of the Hebrew Scriptures written not long after the time of Jesus). Edersheim points out that shepherding was generally viewed with suspicion by rabbinic teaching because it was very difficult to make sure sheep would not steal the property of others by grazing on someone else's land.

But the sacrificial system needed sheep, so Bethlehem, located not far from, and on the road to, Jerusalem tolerated sheepherding.

This sort of information is not just relevant to Jesus's birthplace. You will soon see that if you pay close attention to details such as the occupations of the people Jesus talks to and the locations at which He has those conversations, whole new dimensions of understanding will open before your eyes.

Not paying attention to occupation and location (and other details of context) amounts to underestimating Jesus's knowledge of His location and time. Either He was a sophisticated and well-informed person or He was not. Either He was familiar with the life of the nation, with current affairs, with the way people lived and worked, or He was not.

The truth is He was indeed a knowledgeable person, as His commentaries make clear over and over again. His business parables are true to life in that the numbers correspond to the quantities and orders of magnitude we see in the archeological records of ancient Galilee. His political references evince a knowledge of the politics of the day and an awareness of current events. To ignore the social, economic, and political context in which Jesus spoke is to believe He did not speak in ways fit for the context, as if He did not know where He was and to whom He was speaking.

Before we jump into all that and begin to read Jesus as though He understood His time and place, we must first fend off a possible misunderstanding. When I have spoken to people about this, from time to time I found they'd fallen prey to a false dichotomy, a belief that economic interpretations compete with and cancel out theological interpretations. That is false. There is nothing about putting the Gospels into historical contexts that is at variance with sound theology, unspiritual, or impious. In fact, historic orthodox Christian doctrines require us to take history seriously when studying the Bible.

Is It Unspiritual to Think Jesus Talked About Economics?

One of the things that might stop you from seeing the economic dimension in the Gospel accounts is the idea some have that Jesus only came to talk about "spiritual things," by which they mean nonmaterial things. I see this as a problem especially for my fellow conservatives, which is partly in reaction to the fear of falling into some form of liberalism. But we have nothing to fear from seeing and hearing everything Jesus shows and tells us in the Gospel accounts. In order to do that, however, we need to take off some of our habitual hermeneutical (interpretive) blinders.

When Christian scholars talk about the Gospels, they have tended to focus on theological questions. His divine nature, His incarnation as a human, the relationship between the human and the divine in Him, the nature of His atonement on the cross, the meaning of His resurrection, and the nature of His coming again.

These topics are all about what God intended. Why the Father sent the Son. Why the Son came. What the Son set out to do. Theology tends to focus on God's actions and intentions, as is proper.

But God is not the only character acting in the Gospel accounts. Others act as well. Tax collectors, rabbis, Herodians, Romans each had their own deeds to do, their own different purposes to pursue, things like money, power, and survival.

When we look at their power bases, their interests, plans, and intentions, attention to such historical forces does not in any way contradict the theological truth about God's overall intentions.

Here is an example: The Gospels clearly imply the temple elite wanted Jesus killed because He became a threat to their economic and political positions (you'll hear more about this later on). That fact is perfectly consistent with the fact that Jesus had a higher intention, a plan to turn their evil act to a good purpose.

For some strange reason people sometimes think economic explanations of Jesus's death cancel out theological ones. I once explained to someone why I thought Jesus was killed partly because Rome was in the midst of a financial crisis and Pontius Pilate was too politically weakened by that to stand up to the demands of the Judean mobs. He countered that Jesus was killed because He was the Lamb of God slain before the foundation of the world—as if those two things could not be true at the same time. As if the Roman financial crisis did not occur precisely because Jesus's slaying was decreed before the foundation of the world. Historically informed Gospel reading is not a denial of the foundational theological truths of Christianity.

In fact, I would argue the exact opposite: the fundamental Christian doctrine of the incarnation requires us to see His humanity operating fully in the Gospel accounts, and His humanity includes His human culture and background.

When He took into Himself a human nature, He took into Himself features of humanity with the single exception of sin. He did not just take on a human body (that's a heretical view), He took on a human soul, which includes human relationships: familial, political, cultural, and economic.

The two ancient creeds that laid out the fundamental teaching of the incarnation are the Athanasian Creed and the Chalcedonian Creed. They hold that the Son took on both a human body and a human mind. Here's what the Chalcedonian Creed says Jesus was:

> ...*perfect in Godhead and also perfect in manhood; truly God and truly man, of a reasonable (rational) soul and body; consubstantial (coessential) with the Father according to the Godhead, and consubstantial with us according to the Manhood; in all things like unto us, without sin....*

Other than our sinful nature, He is "in all things like unto us." He took on a body and a mind, and a family, and a nation, and all the social and economic bonds people have. This view is not heresy; it is orthodoxy. The denial of it is heresy.

Now that we have established the theological legitimacy, even the necessity of taking things like economic context into account, next we'll take a deeper dive into some of those details to see how they help us understand Jesus better.

PART II

JESUS: AN ECONOMIC
BIOGRAPHY

Jesus of Nazareth

It mattered that Jesus came from Nazareth. The Bible does not treat the location of His upbringing as a pointless detail. In fact, the Bible gives Jesus's connection with Nazareth a great deal of emphasis.

Christians believe God the Father sent His eternal Son to live as a human being in the world. This doctrine is called the Incarnation, and it is one of the basics of the faith. Less well known is God intentionally planned the cultural and political circumstances of the incarnation of His Son. Did God choose wisely, or would any old time and place have done? The Scriptures say it was carefully planned:

> *...and came and resided in a city called Nazareth, that what was spoken through the prophets might be fulfilled, "He shall be called a Nazarene."*
>
> —MATTHEW 2:23–3:1

None of the times and circumstances of Jesus's birth, growth, and life were accidental details:

But when the fullness of the time came, God sent forth His Son, born of a woman, born under the Law, to redeem those under the Law...

—Galatians 4:4

That includes the fact Jesus grew up in the province of Galilee, in which the village of Nazareth was located.

And leaving Nazareth, he came and dwelt in Capernaum, which is upon the sea coast, in the borders of Zabulon and Nephthalim:

That it might be fulfilled which was spoken by Esaias the prophet, saying,

The land of Zabulon, and the land of Nephthalim, by the way of the sea, beyond Jordan, Galilee of the Gentiles;

The people which sat in darkness saw great light; and to them which sat in the region and shadow of death light is sprung up.

—Matthew 4:13–16 (KJV)

Galilee is very important to the Gospel accounts. Galilee, including also Galilean(s), receives explicit mentions in sixty-five verses of the Gospels. Jesus is associated with Galilee repeatedly by Judeans, and His followers were identified by their distinctive Galilean accents. The characters in these accounts recognized the importance of these regional tensions; we should too.

His origin in Galilee is a consistent theme in the life of Jesus. Almost all the twelve disciples appear to have come from Galilee (though conspicuously the one who betrayed Him appears to be the single exception; he was from Judea, not Galilee). Therefore, it is important to understand Galilee better. Situated in the north of ancient Israel, it was distinct from Judea in almost every way: ethnically, religiously, politically, (as we've seen) linguistically, and (most important for our purposes) economically from Judea in the south.

The distinctive history of Galilee gave it a frontier quality. Religiously conservative and risk-taking, Galilee was crisscrossed by important trade routes connecting the east with the Mediterranean.

This gave Galilee a certain economic dynamism, and though it was less wealthy than Judea, it was on the way up. It was significantly more decentralized than the economies to the south, with a lower tax burden and less centralized state power than Judea with its dependence on Jerusalem, the political and religious center of the region.

Throughout the entire Roman Empire, urbanites saw rural dwellers as nearly subhuman. Though no part of that culture had a full reciprocity between city and country, the evidence shows Galilee had more mutual respect than the norm.

The Great Plain to the south was dominated by gigantic agricultural combines of vast scale apportioned out, often, in acts of political favoritism from Caesar or from the Herodian dynasty. But Galilean agriculture was made up largely of "freehold" farms, owned by the same people who worked them.

Galilee also had small industry as a substantial part of its economic base. Stone jars from Galilee have been found throughout the region, and the fishing villages around the Sea of Galilee did not just catch, dry, and export fish, they also manufactured and exported fishing implements.

Some Galilean cities such as Tiberias and particularly Sepphoris became market centers for regional products, foreign trade, and also financial transactions. Jesus grew up near Sepphoris, which was within easy walking distance from Nazareth. It is almost certain He, a skilled builder, would have worked in the major building boom that occurred in Sepphoris during Jesus's young adulthood.

Obsolete Biblical scholarship (that is, scholarship that has not kept up with archeological findings) continues to paint a picture of Jesus as the product of mass landless poverty, leading a peasant revolt. Recently, archeologists have unearthed a great deal of Galilee, including Nazareth. There were reasonably prosperous villages and, in the case of Sepphoris, prosperous enough to afford luxury goods, art, and even a respectable mansion or two. Nothing in Galilee has been seen that is as opulent as could be found among the ruling class environs of Jerusalem, but the evidence is this trading and financial center was able to generate prosperity, but prosperity based more on commercial enterprise than on political connection and extraction.

This divergence between the relatively dynamic and entrepreneurial economy in which Jesus spent His formative years and the comparatively top-heavy, political economy of Judea provides a backdrop that sheds light on the rest of the Gospel accounts. Jesus never has a single confrontation about wealth while in Galilee. Every one of His confrontations over wealth occurs in or near Judea, and they grow in intensity as He comes closer to and finally enters Jerusalem, the seat of political power.

Jesus, the Galilean by the design of His Father, consistently critiques the centralized, politicized, crony economy He encounters in the capital city, and not the decentralized entrepreneurial economy of His native region.

Jesus learned about the economy from His Scriptures, the Old Testament, but not just from the Old Testament, but also from His neighbors, His friends, His apprenticeship under Joseph the carpenter, and, yes, even from His mother, who had very strong ideas about economics. We'll learn about the economic views of the mother of Jesus next.

The Economic Philosophy of the Virgin Mary

Looking at the economic statements of the Virgin Mary and her influence on her son, Jesus, is fraught with landmines. The most dangerous one goes off when orthodox Christians forget the importance of the fact that under the doctrine of the incarnation, Jesus is both God *and man.*

This danger comes about in reaction to liberal theology. Liberals have historically been skeptical about the divinity of Jesus and have therefore focused only on His humanity. They have engaged in many quests for "the historical Jesus," which really means the quest for a Jesus other than the one found in the Gospels and in orthodox

Christian theology. Because of this liberal emphasis on Jesus's humanity, we conservatives overreact and assume anyone who talks about Jesus's humanity must be denying His divinity. This is, of course, the wrong reaction.

The only real option for Christians is to acknowledge Jesus is both God and man. But if He is a man, He had a mother. Did He listen to His mother? Did He love His mother? Did He learn from His mother? Of course He did. That's what sons do—they learn from their parents.

What does "honor your father and mother" mean? It means many things, and one of them is to learn from your father and your mother. The Bible repeatedly points to the parental function as one of teaching (Deuteronomy 6; Proverbs 1). If Jesus was a good son, He learned from His parents. If God had the wisdom to choose a good mother for His son, then Mary was somebody worth learning from.

But did Jesus learn at all? Of course He did.

And Jesus kept increasing in wisdom and stature, and in favor with God and men.

—Luke 2:52

If that verse seems strange to you, it just goes to show how very much the true doctrine of the incarnation has fallen into obscurity. If Jesus is fully man, of course He'd get smarter over time. If it seems normal to you that Jesus got taller but not that He got smarter, then you might have fallen into the heresy of Apollinarianism, which is the view that Jesus had a human body, but only a divine mind. That heresy is wrong. Jesus was a human body and mind in unity with divinity.

What sorts of things did Jesus learn from other people? All sorts of things, including things about economics. He learned how to make an economic living from His foster father, Joseph. How do we know this? Joseph was a carpenter and so was Jesus.

Did He learn anything about economics from His mother? Of course He did. She had strong economic views. He had strong economic views. His economic views were so similar to hers, His views were very nearly quotes from her. And, finally, she was His mother, and people tend to learn their economic and political philosophy from their parents, especially premodern people.

Okay, with that distraction (hopefully) behind us, let's talk about her economic views.

Mary's cousin, Elizabeth, conceived John the Baptist before Mary conceived Jesus. After Mary conceived, she traveled from Galilee south to Judea where Elizabeth lived.

Now at this time Mary arose and went with haste to the hill country, to a city of Judah, and entered the house of Zacharias and greeted Elizabeth.

—Luke 1:39–40

Elizabeth's child, John, while still in the womb leapt for joy at the coming of his younger cousin, Jesus, also in the womb.

And it came about that when Elizabeth heard Mary's greeting, the baby leaped in her womb;...

—Luke 1:41

Elizabeth felt that physical leap and responded with her own rhetorical leap of faith and joy.

...and Elizabeth was filled with the Holy Spirit.

And she cried out with a loud voice, and said, "Blessed among women are you, and blessed is the fruit of your womb!

And how has it happened to me, that the mother of my Lord should come to me?"

—Luke 1:41–43

That statement was revolutionary. Elizabeth and her husband, Zacharias, were socioeconomically above Mary and her husband, Joseph. Elizabeth and Zacharias's son, John, would be socioeconomically above Mary and Joseph's son, Jesus.

In what ways was Elizabeth of higher status than Mary? First, Mary was from Galilee, from the small village of Nazareth. Galilee was of lower status than Judea, and Nazareth was viewed as of lower status than other parts of Galilee.

The next day He purposed to go forth into Galilee, *and He found Philip. And Jesus said to him, "Follow Me."*

Now Philip was from Bethsaida, *of the city of Andrew and Peter.*

Philip found Nathanael and said to him, "We have found Him of whom Moses in the Law and also the Prophets wrote, Jesus of Naza-reth, the son of Joseph."

And Nathanael said to him, "Can any good thing come out of Nazareth?"

—JOHN 1:43–46 (emphases mine)

So, Mary was from a lower-status village of a lower-status province than Elizabeth.

In addition, Mary was the wife of a carpenter, whereas Elizabeth was the wife of a priest. And not just a priest, a priest of such standing as to be on the rotation to offer incense offerings in the Holy Place of the Temple, an event that drew large crowds.

...there was a certain priest named Zacharias, of the division of Abijah; and he had a wife from the daughters of Aaron, and her name was Elizabeth.... Now it came about, while he was performing his priestly service before God in the appointed order of his division, according to the custom of the priestly office, he was chosen by lot to enter the temple of the Lord and burn incense. And the whole multitude *of the people were in prayer outside at the hour of the incense offering.*

—LUKE 1:5–10 (emphasis mine)

Not only did Elizabeth marry into a priestly family, she was a descendant of the original high priest. Yes, Joseph was a descendant of King David, but so was Zacharias, via his ancestor, Abijah. So both families had Davidic roots (they were related after all), but in that present time, the status of a priestly family from Judea and in the rotation to serve inside the holy place of the temple ranked well above the family from Nazareth whose man of the house pounded nails for a living.

High-ranking priests would be considerably financially wealthier as well.

Despite her higher wealth and status, Elizabeth, "filled with the Holy Spirit," declares both Mary and Jesus's superiority, expressing wonder that they should even "come to" or visit her.

Elizabeth's son, John, later expresses the same inversion of status.

The next day he saw Jesus coming to him and said, "Behold, the Lamb of God who takes away the sin of the world! This is He on behalf of whom I said, 'After me comes a Man who has a higher rank than I, for He existed before me.'"

—JOHN 1:29-30

John's surprise at Jesus's coming to him to be baptized and John's statement of unworthiness is parallel to his mother's reaction to the visit from Mary and the unborn Jesus. Apparently, Jesus was not the only prophet in the family who was influenced by His mother.

Mary saw the socially revolutionary nature of Elizabeth's response and responded to it with her own complimentary prophetic poem, known to history as the Magnificat, which hits on the same theme of reversal of class and status, but in much greater detail.

And Mary said: "My soul exalts the Lord,
    And my spirit has rejoiced in God my Savior.
    For He has had regard for the humble state of His bondslave;
    For behold, from this time on all generations will count me blessed.
    For the Mighty One has done great things for me; And holy is His name.
    And His mercy is upon generation after generation Toward those who fear Him.

He has done mighty deeds with His arm; He has scattered those who were proud in the thoughts of their heart.

He has brought down rulers from their thrones, And has exalted those who were humble.

He has filled the hungry with good things; *And* sent away the rich empty-*handed.*

He has given help to Israel His servant, In remembrance of His mercy,

As He spoke to our fathers, To Abraham and his offspring forever."

—LUKE 1:46–55 (emphasis mine)

Try to set aside pious habit and medieval tradition (or reaction to medieval tradition) for just a moment and see how shockingly this-worldly the Magnificat is. There is almost nothing here about heaven, arguably no direct reference at all. It's much more Hebraic than the much later Marian devotion, and the Hebrew tradition was very focused on what God was going to do in the world, as opposed to out of and after the world.

The core is political and economic. This is not to say the core is not theological. It is more to say it is economic and political theology; theology about how God was going to intervene and tear down hierarchies of wealth and power. If you have a knee-jerk reaction that sees this as pushing some kind of socialist agenda, let me remind you that socialism sets up political and economic hierarchies—always. Liberation theology has stolen these passages from us (in the same way it advocates stealing property from farmers). The proper reaction is not to concede the ground to them and acquiesce in their plunder, but rather to take this ground back for Biblical Christianity.

One-third of the text directly addresses sociopolitical change, and that third sheds a lot of light on the rest of the text, like verses 51–53, as well as the meaning of "humble state" in verse 48. In light of this, "the Mighty One has done great things for me" probably refers partly to upending of the social order.

Even her reference to Abraham is put in a new possible light when we remember all his life, including his encounters with political and economic tyranny: his mistreatment by Pharaoh, his mistreatment by Abimelech, and his rescue of Lot from being kidnapped and enslaved by the political hegemony of the region at the time.

Let's deal with the issue of hyperspiritualizing this passage.

Otherworldly schools of Christianity have done a lot of spiritualizing this economic commentary away, as if the scattering of the proud and the sending away empty of the rich are always going on in our hearts or something like that. But that won't do. Mary emphasizes the historically unique moment this represented, as the final fulfillment of deferred promise "to our fathers, to Abraham and his offspring...."

It's not a perennial fortune cookie kind of thing; it is about what her Son would repeatedly call "this generation." Not all the generations before. Not all the generations after. Not after the end of the world. At that time in history.

Given what we've already said about the doctrine of the incarnation and Mary's obviously strong views about politics and economics, it should surprise no one if we find Mary's economic philosophy had a major impact on Jesus and His teaching.

The Gospels show her influence on Him in the incident of the wedding at Cana, and Joseph is not mentioned after the incident at the temple when Jesus was twelve, which suggests even more of a maternal influence.

As I mentioned in the introduction to this book, there is a consistent geographical pattern to Jesus's economic discourse: no confrontations occurred over wealth while in Galilee—all of them occur in or near Judea, particularly in close proximity to Jerusalem. This geographical pattern started with His mother. Her conversation with the angel Gabriel occurs while she is in Galilee and has nothing explicit to say about economic matters. All of that waits upon her visit to Elizabeth in, yes, Judea. Remember:

Now at this time Mary arose and went with haste to the hill country, to a city of Judah, and entered the house of Zacharias and greeted Elizabeth.

—LUKE 1:39-40

The parallel goes beyond geography, though. Take a close look at Jesus's Sermon on the Plain and you'll see clear evidence of Mary:

Blessed are you who hunger now, for you shall be satisfied. *Blessed are you who weep now, for you shall laugh....*

But woe to you who are rich, for you are receiving your comfort in full.

Woe to you who are well-fed now, for you shall be hungry. *Woe to you who laugh now, for you shall mourn and weep.*

—LUKE 6:21-25 (emphasis mine)

Look at the statements side by side:

Magnificat	Sermon on the Plain
filled the hungry with good things	who hunger now, for you shall be satisfied
sent away the rich empty	woe to you who are rich, for you are receiving your comfort in full. Woe to you who are well-fed now, for you shall be hungry.

Mary had basis in her own personal experience to see the ruling class of ancient Israel as economically exploitative, and to see that if God chose someone like her to bear the Messiah, that represented a reversal.

First, we see the nativity narrative begins with the description of economic exploitation:

And it came to pass in those days, that there went out a decree from Caesar Augustus, that all the world should be taxed.

—LUKE 2:1 (KJV)

The enrollment (for the purpose of taxation) imposed enormous costs on this young family. Aside from the tax, there was what accountants now call "compliance cost," meaning the destruction of value in actually going about the process of payment. We grumble about filling out complicated tax forms (and understandably so), but imagine if the process of calculating tax liability involved multiweek travel on foot along primitive and dangerous roads. Loss of comfort; loss of wages; expenses of travel; risk of life and limb. And, in this case, with a late-term pregnant woman.

And this couple did not have a lot of economic margin. Although Nazareth was not the poverty case it has often been portrayed as (more on the economic status of Nazareth later), neither was it affluent.

More to the point, Mary and Joseph were the victims of economic exploitation by the ruling class:

> *And when eight days were completed before His circumcision, His name was then called Jesus, the name given by the angel before He was conceived in the womb. And when the days for their purification according to the law of Moses were completed, they brought Him up to Jerusalem to present Him to the Lord (as it is written in the Law of the Lord, "Every first-born male that opens the womb shall be called holy to the Lord"), and to offer a sacrifice according to what was said in the Law of the Lord, "A pair of turtledoves, or two young pigeons."*
>
> *—Luke 2:21–24*

The law permitted those who cannot "afford a lamb"—literally "get" a lamb—to offer a pair of turtledoves or pigeons as an alternative sacrifice.

> *Then he shall offer it before the LORD and make atonement for her; and she shall be cleansed from the flow of her blood. This is the law for her who bears a child, whether a male or a female. But if she cannot afford a lamb, then she shall take two turtledoves or two young*

pigeons, the one for a burnt offering and the other for a sin offering; and the priest shall make atonement for her, and she shall be clean.

—Leviticus 12:7–8

This law was supposed to help the poor, to lower the burden of the "unfunded mandate" of sacrifice on them. Except the problem is the priestly class modified the law in such a way as to exploit those who participated in it. The system was gamed out in such a way that the process of currency exchange, which was required of those purchasing sacrificial animals, involved a two-for-one exchange rate. This means there was a 100 percent premium on switching from the currency held by the typical Israelite to the required temple currency. As a result, worshippers paid double to participate in the system.

Since the sacrifice of turtledoves was designated for those with little or no economic margin, who were least able to withstand the exploitation, it was especially exploitative. As we will see below, this is the reason we see the adult Jesus forcefully confront those selling animals for sacrifice and singling out the dove merchants in particular.

Who benefited from this system? The beneficiaries were the royal and the priestly class, the class to which cousin Elizabeth and Zacharias belonged. All those young carpenters' families and farmers and stonemasons and day laborers sacrificed as currency markups accumulated in the pockets of the temple elite. And Elizabeth, a member of that class, had just confessed the primacy of Jesus and His bearer.

Mary saw what it meant and put it in a prophetic poem and told Luke about it (or someone who told it to him), and he wrote it down for the ages. Of course, Jesus would have known about all of that and of course it helped form who He was, alerting Him to the ways in which bureaucracies that are supposed to be performing functions designed to help the poor, in reality end up hurting them.

Bethlehem Steal

The story of the nativity in Bethlehem is the story of government plundering people of their wealth.

> *Now it came about in those days that a decree went out from Caesar Augustus, that a census be taken of all the inhabited earth.*
>
> *This was the first census taken while Quirinius was governor of Syria.*
>
> *And all were proceeding to register for the census, everyone to his own city.*
>
> *And Joseph also went up from Galilee, from the city of Nazareth, to Judea, to the city of David, which is called Bethlehem, because he was of the house and family of David....*

—LUKE 2:1-4

The King James version makes clearer what the census was for:

> *And it came to pass in those days, that there went out a decree from Caesar Augustus, that all the world should be taxed.*

—LUKE 2:1 (KJV)

That's because the word the Bible uses for "census," *apographo*, although it literally refers to an act of writing, when viewed in the historical context, implies the purpose is taxation. That was the purpose of a Roman census at that time.

The passage has been the subject of much debate. Critics of the accuracy of the Bible point out that Quirinius was not governor of Syria until well after the time of Jesus's birth. However, leading New Testament scholar N. T. Wright argues persuasively that the proper translation is these events occurred "before Quirinius was governor of Syria."

But the anti-scriptural polemic angle, in addition to being easily answered, distracts from a very real and important issue: Why mention Quirinius, governor of Syria at all? Why would it matter who would be in charge of a neighboring state? Because the Gospel writer knows that after Jesus's birth, and after His attempted murder by Herod, the Herodian dynasty would lose power due to incompetence and corruption, and Israel would be placed under the jurisdiction of Syria.

As our argument unfolds, we'll see that Jesus is frequently at odds with the ruling class, and the ruling class of the ruling class are the Herodians. From the very beginning they are shown as both vicious and craven. The nativity narrative starts with Caesar Augustus, not Herod. Caesar decides to impose a census. Herod is not mentioned, despite the fact that the story we're about to read about Mary and Joseph and the birth of Jesus takes place entirely in Herod's jurisdiction. The only reference we get to the mighty Herod "the Great," who is not even consulted about a census proceeding within his own border, is a no-name appearance and a not-too-subtle reminder that the Herods would shortly be demoted to last-among-equals subservience to the Roman appointee in charge of Israel's northern neighbor.

We don't know much historical detail about the particular tax imposed here. The New Testament is the only historical reference to this particular act of enrollment, though we do have information about others. Acts 5 mentions another tax-based enrollment. What is most likely is this was a poll tax, meaning a tax on individuals. That and property taxes would be the typical reasons for such a survey.

As far as we know, women were not required to make a pilgrimage back to ancestral homes. This raises the question as to why Mary traveled with Joseph. This has sometimes been raised as an objection against the historicity of the Gospel account. But as per usual, these objections not only fail to refute the Bible, they tend to block commentators from searching for deeper meanings. There was a perfectly good reason for Joseph to bring Mary, even without legal requirement to do so: to save her life. Few would believe her story about divine conception. She would have been vulnerable to vigilante violence against her for pregnancy outside of marriage. Given that risk, it makes perfect sense for her to be brought on the trip, even one as difficult as a long pilgrimage while in late stage pregnancy. All this occurs in an economic context. Israel was subjugated. Its kings failed to rule justly. Its people were under bondage to a foreign power and were subject to the whims of the state. This is hardly an auspicious start for anyone who would use the Gospel accounts to argue in favor of centralization of political power and growth of the state. It is the overgrown state of Rome and the corrupt and incompetent state of Jerusalem that stand condemned in this account. But Rome gets less of the sharp end of the pen than Jerusalem. As we shall see, Jerusalem will be disturbed by hearing of the birth of her Messiah.

Before that, let's learn a little bit about the economic base of Jesus's birthplace, Bethlehem. It was not a place of prominence:

> And when Herod the king heard it, he was troubled, and all Jerusalem with him.
>
> And gathering together all the chief priests and scribes of the people, he began to inquire of them where the Christ was to be born.
>
> And they said to him, "In Bethlehem of Judea, for so it has been written by the prophet,
>
> 'And you, Bethlehem, land of Judah, Are by no means least among the leaders of Judah; For out of you shall come forth a Ruler, Who will shepherd My people Israel.'"

—MATTHEW 2:3–6

This reputation goes back to the very first mention of Bethlehem in the Bible, the death of Jacob's wife, Rachel, in childbirth:

> So Rachel died and was buried on the way to Ephrath (that is, Bethlehem).
>
> And Jacob set up a pillar over her grave; that is the pillar of Rachel's grave to this day.
>
> Then Israel journeyed on and pitched his tent beyond the tower of Eder.

—GENESIS 35:19–21

Then there is a gruesome story in Judges 19 about a Levite from Bethlehem who committed simony and concubinage and then left his concubine to be raped and murdered, after which, he dismembered her. Bethlehem is also the central geographical point in the generally tragic account we find in the book of Ruth. Yes, things ended well for Ruth, but the story begins with a famine and then the sudden tragic death of Bethlehemite emigres. Bethlehem was not a locus of fond memories. We associate it with Christmas pageants. They associated it with women dying in childbirth. We think of Christmas cookies. They thought of famine.

The Gospel writer is aware of this association, which is why he quotes Jeremiah's lament about the death of Rachel in response to the Slaughter of the Innocents in Bethlehem:

Then that which was spoken through Jeremiah the prophet was fulfilled, saying,

"A voice was heard in Ramah, Weeping and great mourning, Rachel weeping for her children; And she refused to be comforted, Because they were no more."

—MATTHEW 2:17-18

But God is the God of reversals, so the prophet Micah predicts that despite Bethlehem being among the least of the cities of Israel (probably in size and reputation), it would become great:

But as for you, Bethlehem Ephrathah, Too little to be among the clans of Judah, From you One will go forth for Me to be ruler in Israel. His goings forth are from long ago, From the days of eternity.

Therefore, He will give them up until the time When she who is in labor has borne a child. Then the remainder of His brethren Will return to the sons of Israel.

—MICAH 5:2-3

Please note that Micah even alludes to labor and childbirth, a clear signal he was aware of the tragedy of the death of Rachel. As we saw above, Matthew's Gospel pulls all this together and quotes Micah in the context of the birth of Jesus. (Matthew 2:3–6)

Jesus was not born in Bethlehem because it was great. He was born in Bethlehem because it was notorious. God starts the healing where things are most broken. We'll see a bit later how this same pattern is identified by the prophets and quoted by the Gospels in explaining why God had Jesus raised in Galilee.

There's one more important point to make about Bethlehem and its poor reputation, and this point is directly tied to its economic base. Bethlehem was a designated dumping zone for a despised, but necessary, occupation—shepherding. Not just shepherding as such, but the raising specifically of sheep for the temple sacrifices. The great Jewish convert Alfred Edersheim has the story:

> ...Jewish tradition may here prove both illustrative and helpful. That the Messiah was to be born in Bethlehem, was a settled conviction. Equally so was the belief, that He was to be revealed from Migdal Eder, "the tower of the flock." This Migdal Eder was not the watchtower for the ordinary flocks which pastured on the barren sheep ground beyond Bethlehem, but lay close to the town, on the road to Jerusalem. A passage in the Mishnah leads to the conclusion that the flocks, which pastured there, were destined for Temple-sacrifices, and, accordingly, that the shepherds, who watched over them, were not ordinary shepherds. The latter were under the ban of Rabbinism, on account of their necessary isolation from religious ordinances, and their manner of life, which rendered strict legal observance unlikely, if not absolutely impossible.[1]

That's right. The Lamb of God who takes away the sin of the world was born in the village that was set aside specifically for the purpose of breeding and exporting to Jerusalem lambs of God for the sacrifice. But this is both a positive and a negative association. He is the unspotted Lamb, a positive. But as we will see over and over again, He comes from a despised place, in this case the center of shepherding, barely tolerated by tradition, which is nevertheless necessary to the operation of the ruling class and its revenue center in the Jerusalem temple.

Herod's Philosophy of Economics

Have you ever noticed this little detail from the Gospel of Matthew? The wise men foresaw the birth of the Messiah and, when that happened, not just Herod was troubled, but all Jerusalem was troubled too.

> *Now after Jesus was born in Bethlehem of Judea in the days of Herod the king, behold, magi from the east arrived in Jerusalem, saying,*
> *"Where is He who has been born King of the Jews? For we saw His star in the east, and have come to worship Him." And when Herod the king heard it, he was troubled, and all Jerusalem with him.*
>
> —MATTHEW 2:1–3 (emphasis mine)

What would bother Jerusalem about the coming of the Messiah? Sure, it makes sense that Herod, an unpopular tyrant who was known for his paranoia about rivals, would be on alert. He even had his own sons murdered to avoid challenges to his power. The Messiah would be a threat to Herod. But why was all Jerusalem feeling the same anxiety? It is not a given that Jerusalem would be disturbed by this announcement; it's "good news."

Let's take a closer look at the prophecy scholars used to show the Messiah would come from Bethlehem.

> *But as for you, Bethlehem Ephrathah, Too little to be among the clans of Judah, From you One will go forth for Me to be ruler in Israel. His goings forth are from long ago, From the days of eternity.*
>
> *Therefore, He will give them up until the time When she who is in labor has borne a child. Then the remainder of His brethren Will return to the sons of Israel.*
>
> *And* He will arise and shepherd His flock In the strength of the LORD, *In the majesty of the name of the LORD His God.* And

they *will remain, Because at that time He will be* great To the ends of the earth.

And this One will be our peace.

—MICAH 5:2–5 (emphases mine)

It's filled with glad tidings indeed: good for Judaism and for the world. God would be "great to the ends of the earth" and He "will be our peace." What's the problem?

The problem was the system then was good for Jerusalem's ruling class, but bad for everyone else.

We have shown above and will show below in even greater detail that Jerusalem was a city sustained by economic exploitation of the rest of Israel. The coming of the Messiah was a classic good news/bad news situation: Good news for the world—the Messiah would bring justice; bad news for Jerusalem for exactly the same reason.

Economic exploitation is usually built on a scarcity philosophy that falsely holds that the only way to win is at the expense of someone else. That is what led Herod, as well as many despots before and after him, to genocidal actions.

Then when Herod saw that he had been tricked by the magi, he became very enraged, and sent and slew all the male children who were in Bethlehem and in all its environs, *from two years old and under, according to the time which he had ascertained from the magi.*

—MATTHEW 2:16 (emphasis mine)

As any student of the Bible can plainly see, Herod, although allegedly the king of the Jews, is acting like the pharaoh described in the book of Exodus. The Exodus pharaoh also adhered to a system of economic extraction that was built on zero-sum economics, and that economic thinking also led him to genocide, particularly the mass murder of Hebrew children. Herod was just a smaller-scale pharaoh, a mass killer of young Hebrew boys.

That explains why the escape of Joseph, Mary, and Jesus from Israel to Egypt is described as a fulfillment of a prophecy about the Exodus, and in a way that subversively upends the geography:

> Now when they had departed, behold, an angel of the Lord appeared to Joseph in a dream, saying, "Arise and take the Child and His mother, and flee to Egypt, and remain there until I tell you; for Herod is going to search for the Child to destroy Him."
>
> And he arose and took the Child and His mother by night, and departed for Egypt;
>
> and was there until the death of Herod, that what was spoken by the Lord through the prophet might be fulfilled, saying, "Out of Egypt did I call My Son."
>
> —MATTHEW 2:12–15 (emphasis mine)

Note how the geography is reappropriated by Matthew. Jesus was not actually going from Egypt to Israel, like in the original context. He was making the opposite trip, from Israel to Egypt. But now their roles were reversed. Israel's king was acting like Egypt's pharaoh had acted a millennium and a half before. Egypt became the safe place of escape for a Hebrew baby. Israel was the new Egypt. This would not be the last time the New Testament touches upon this theme; it was the first of many.

I wrote earlier about how the economic pronouncements of Mary implied she thought Jesus would somehow initiate a disruption of the corrupt economic order. She saw the arrogant ruling class possibly being driven from power. In a sense, Herod agreed with her conclusions, but he was looking at things from the other side of the tracks. Herod and Mary both agreed the coming of the Messiah would be an earth-shattering event for the rulers of Israel; they simply disagreed about whether that was a desirable outcome.

Herod, with his finely tuned survival instinct, was able to discern something many otherworldly Christians have not seen: The Messiah would change more than just hearts and souls; He would upend the nations and their rulers. He did not just come to change who the rulers were—He came to change the rules themselves. Herod's tyranny, held in place by power and by mass employment of workers in his string of public works projects, was threatened by the coming of the Messiah, the true King.

The Thousand-Year-Old Economic Grudge

Before we plunge into some of the economic detail associated with the geopolitics of Jesus's time, let's stop for a deeper look into what was already ancient history by the time of Jesus: the deep split between Judea and the north. The division between Judea and the provinces north of it was based on rifts that occurred almost a thousand years before the time of Jesus. It all goes back to the time of Jesus's ancestor, King Solomon.

Solomon died and his son Rehoboam became the king of a united Israel. Solomon had centralized power by moving away from a system of independent tribes to a system of appointed districts. He had also embarked on a major spending project, one ordered by God. He built up Jerusalem by building, among other things, a compound that included both palace complex and the temple. This was an expensive endeavor, and it required heavy taxation. But since God had instructed Solomon to build the temple complex, it was necessary.

However, after Solomon's building boom and his life on earth were completed, the taxing and spending remained high. The tribes of Israel approached the new king asking for relief.

Then Rehoboam went to Shechem, for all Israel had come to Shechem to make him king.

Now it came about when Jeroboam the son of Nebat heard of it, that he was living in Egypt (for he was yet in Egypt, where he had fled from the presence of King Solomon).

Then they sent and called him, and Jeroboam and all the assembly of Israel came and spoke to Rehoboam, saying,

"Your father made our yoke hard; now therefore lighten the hard service of your father and his heavy yoke which he put on us, and we will serve you."

—Kings 12:1–4

Rehoboam had two sets of advisors: those with older, grayer, presumably wiser heads, whom he inherited from his father, and younger, foolish advisors who were part of his own circle of friends.

He consulted his father's advisors first:

And King Rehoboam consulted with the elders who had served his father Solomon while he was still alive, saying, "How do you counsel me to answer this people?"

Then they spoke to him, saying, "If you will be a servant to this people today, will serve them, grant them their petition, and speak good words to them, then they will be your servants forever."

—1 Kings 12:6–7

Apparently, he did not like that advice, so he looked for other counsel.

But he forsook the counsel of the elders which they had given him, and consulted with the young men who grew up with him and served him.

So he said to them, "What counsel do you give that we may answer this people who have spoken to me, saying, 'Lighten the yoke which your father put on us'?"

—1 Kings 12:8–9

The young advisors gave him the opposite advice from the elder ones.

And the young men who grew up with him spoke to him, saying, "Thus you shall say to this people who spoke to you, saying, 'Your father made our yoke heavy, now you make it lighter for us!' But you shall speak to them, 'My little finger is thicker than my father's loins! Whereas my father loaded you with a heavy yoke, I will add to your

30

yoke; my father disciplined you with whips, but I will discipline you with scorpions.'"

—1 KINGS 12:10–11

Rehoboam liked his friends' advice and he enacted it.

Then Jeroboam and all the people came to Rehoboam on the third day as the king had directed, saying, "Return to me on the third day." And the king answered the people harshly, for he forsook the advice of the elders which they had given him, and he spoke to them according to the advice of the young men, saying, "My father made your yoke heavy, but I will add to your yoke; my father disciplined you with whips, but I will discipline you with scorpions."

—1 KINGS 12:12–14

The reaction was predictable and has been reproduced many, many times down through history, a tax revolt leading to secession.

When all Israel saw that the king did not listen to them, the people answered the king, saying, "What portion do we have in David? We have no inheritance in the son of Jesse; To your tents, O Israel! Now look after your own house, David!" So Israel departed to their tents.

But as for the sons of Israel who lived in the cities of Judah, Rehoboam reigned over them.

—1 KINGS 12:16–17

This happened circa 930 BC. That would not be the last tax revolt against a central power. And as we will see in the life of Jesus, it will not be the last time economic tension would exist between the north and the south of Israel.

So, the northern ten tribes seceded, and Judah (with a tiny remnant Benjamin absorbed into it) became a separate nation. And the issue was one of centralization of power and economic exploitation. The northern kingdoms went on to form their own nation (something God permitted) and their own religion (something God forbade) and, as a consequence of the latter, they fell under the judgment of God and were captured by the Assyrian empire in roughly 720 BC. Later, the northern tribes fell to the next great empire, Babylon, launching what is known as the Babylonian Captivity.

Eventually, the tribes were released, and many Israelites made their way back to the Holy Land. But the split was not forgotten by the people and certainly not by God. In fact, God promised a special blessing for the northern tribes, which fell under the first (the Assyrian) captivity.

The prophet Isaiah, in the eighth chapter of his eponymous book, predicts Assyria will be judged by God by being conquered by the next empire, Babylon. Babylon would then capture Judah. But then, in a famous Messianic prophecy, God declares through Isaiah:

> But there will be no more gloom for her who was in anguish; in earlier times He treated the land of Zebulun and the land of Naphtali with contempt, but later on He shall make it glorious, by the way of the sea, on the other side of Jordan, Galilee of the Gentiles.
>
> The people who walk in darkness Will see a great light; Those who live in a dark land, The light will shine on them.
>
> —ISAIAH 9:1–2

In other words, though the northern sections, Galilee, and environs suffered first, they also would be first restored.

Mark's Gospel applies this to the ministry of Jesus and the beginning of His preaching the coming of the Kingdom of God.

> Now when He heard that John had been taken into custody, He withdrew into Galilee;
>
> and leaving Nazareth, He came and settled in Capernaum, which is by the sea, in the region of Zebulun and Naphtali.
>
> This was to fulfill what was spoken through Isaiah the prophet, saying,
>
> "The land of Zebulun and the land of Naphtali, By the way of the sea, beyond the Jordan, Galilee of the Gentiles—

"The people who were sitting in darkness saw a great light, And to those who were sitting in the land and shadow of death, Upon them a light dawned."

From that time Jesus began to preach and say, "Repent, for the kingdom of heaven is at hand."

—Matthew 4:12–17

So, the fact the Messiah started His declaration of His earthly reign in the northern region is not a matter of happenstance without reference to the history of Israel. God places that decision in the context of the historical division of Israel into north and south. The first destroyed is the first restored.

But what does a thousand-year-old division have to do with the ministry of the Messiah in the context of economic tension between north and south? Why is what happened in the tenth century BC relevant to what happens in the 1st Century AD?

Well, it's relevant partly because circumstances are similar. When the kingdom of Israel was restored, Jerusalem was once again in charge. Galilee was brutally conquered and subjugated by the Israelite dynasty (which would ultimately be controlled by the Herodians). The temple establishment once again economically exploited the north. The tensions were real in the first century AD, just as they were in the tenth century BC.

In addition, the differences in economic dynamics between the two regions would also hold in Jesus's time.

We know from a careful reading of the prophecies regarding Issachar and Zebulon, the two tribes that roughly constitute what would come to be known as upper and lower Galilee, that Zebulon, which is probably where Nazareth was located and where Jesus grew up, was a commercial tribe.

Jacob's blessing over his sons includes what appears to be a calling in trading and commerce for Zebulon:

Zebulun shall dwell at the seashore; And he shall be a haven for ships, And his flank shall be toward Sidon.

—GENESIS 49:13

Centuries later, Moses gives a similar blessing to what has grown from individual sons into full tribes:

And of Zebulun he said, "Rejoice, Zebulun, in your going forth, And, Issachar, in your tents.

They shall call peoples to the mountain; There they shall offer righteous sacrifices; For they shall draw out the abundance of the seas, And the hidden treasures of the sand."

—DEUTERONOMY 33:18–19

This makes sense topographically. Zebulon abutted the sea and was near to one of the great port cities of the region, Tyre. Upper Galilee was largely mountainous. So, both in the time of the original division of the kingdom and at the time of Jesus, Zebulun/Lower Galilee was the land route from the ancient eastern empires of Persia and Babylon to the ports of the Mediterranean and back. This made it a natural commercial conduit and a place of elevated entrepreneurial activity in both periods. Rabbinical tradition clearly identifies Zebulun as a zone of commerce at the time of the Davidic monarchy (two short generations before the division of the kingdom), and archeological evidence shows this same zone in which Jesus grew up was likewise a trading center and an entrepreneurial culture.

So, as we begin our look at the life of Jesus as seen through the economic lens of the time, we start off knowing there was a long-lasting division between what came to be called Galilee in the north, where Jesus was from, and Judah (renamed in Romanized form, Judea) in the south. The division between north and south was over excess centralization of power and economic exploitation by the ruling class of the capital region. There was also a significant difference in the nature of the two economies. The north was based more on commerce, and the south was based on taxation and the temple as a source of revenues.

As we have already discussed, both the prophecy of Isaiah 9 and the way Mark's Gospel applies that prophecy to the ministry of Jesus reveals God's plan was to have Jesus first declare the coming of the kingdom in Galilee, for a specific reason. The land of Zebulun and Naphtali were destroyed after the division of the kingdom. But God had not forgotten them. In other words, God was consciously taking into account the history of regional differences between the northern and southern kingdoms in His plans for the life of Jesus. The difference was, among other things, the difference between the makers of wealth and the takers of it.

The Galilean

As we've seen, God chose Galilee as the home province of His Son with great care and clearly expressed intent. The choice of Galilee was quite important, and that fact shows in the Gospels. Fully sixty-five verses of the Gospels mention Galilee or Galilean(s). Jesus's origin in Galilee was a recurring theme in His life, and even in the lives of His friends. Peter was identified as a disciple of Jesus due to his Galilean accent.

> Now Peter was sitting outside in the courtyard, and a certain servant-girl came to him and said, "You too were with Jesus the Galilean."
>
> But he denied it before them all, saying, "I do not know what you are talking about."
>
> And when he had gone out to the gateway, another servant-girl saw him and said to those who were there, "This man was with Jesus of Nazareth."
>
> And again he denied it with an oath, "I do not know the man."
>
> And a little later the bystanders came up and said to Peter, "Surely you too are one of them; for the way you talk gives you away."
>
> —MATTHEW 26:69–73

When the Sanhedrin member Nicodemus expresses even a slight sympathy for Jesus, other members bitingly label him as a Galilean.

Nicodemus said to them (he who came to Him before, being one of them), "Our Law does not judge a man, unless it first hears from him and knows what he is doing, does it?"

They answered and said to him, "You are not also from Galilee, are you? Search, and see that no prophet arises out of Galilee."

—JOHN 7:50–52

By the way, their claim was wrong. It's generally agreed that five prophets came from Galilee. The point is not their accuracy, but rather the bias that caused them to stumble in their accuracy. What I call above "the thousand-year-old grudge" was quite active in Jesus's time and ran both ways.

So, what kind of a place was Galilee? And since this is a book about economics, let's focus on what kind of economy it had.

Galilee was quite distinct from Judea. It was under separate political jurisdiction, a fact Pilate tried to use to get rid of the political hot potato of Jesus's trial. The history of this political separation is still being debated, but the most likely account is that Galilee was colonized by Jewish nationalists from Judea. The Judean policy seems to have been to try to extend Jewish culture into the mostly pagan north. These settlers were most likely religious conservatives, but over time became adept at dealing with pagans. They were frontier people, practical and self-reliant.

Because upper Galilee is mountainous, it lacked a developed system of high-volume trading roads. But Lower Galilee had many infrastructure hubs and was a major trading corridor. Jesus grew up fairly close to that major trading thoroughfare.

So, Jesus grew up in and around a commercially vibrant region, a conduit from the ancient empires of the East to the more modern Mediterranean ports that served as connections to Greece and Rome.

Anyone who grew up in Galilee was used to dealing with well-traveled merchants from many types of backgrounds. Galileans, or at least those from lower Galilee, had to be able to deal with Jews, Greeks, Romans, and Parthians, among others. They would have grown up hearing people speaking in multiple languages.

Ancient Mediterranean society tended to be hierarchical. Certainly, as one went south from Nazareth toward Judea, the evidence shows the economy became more and more top down. Galilee was, by contrast, economically and culturally more flat. Especially noteworthy was the relationship between urban, suburban, and rural populations. The general Mediterranean outlook of urban elites was that rural peasants were barely human. But evidence indicates Galilee was different; it enjoyed an unusual level of reciprocity between urban and rural populations. Of course, it would not live up to modern egalitarian rhetoric, but by the standards of the time it seems to have had an unusually high degree of mutual respect; or perhaps more properly, we should say a lower degree of mutual contempt.

Economic organization seems to have been quite different in Galilee as well. According to the most recent archeology, Galilee had many small-farm "freeholders," farmers who owned the farms they worked, anywhere from fifteen to forty acres.

There was also small industry there. Stoneware from Galilee is found throughout Israel (confirmed by the latest nuclear analysis of clay samples). And there was a flourishing industrial fishing sector, not just sustenance fishing for direct consumption, but large-scale fishing for export. Fish were dried and salted and shipped around the empire.

The Galilean economy flourished in a way an economy does when early in its development. Eventually, societies can centralize and ossify, leaving entrepreneurial dynamism behind. But it looks as though Galilee was yet to fall into that state of imperial economic decadence.

In the 1970s and '80s, a lot of biblical scholarship worked on the assumption that Galilee was backward and poor. A common view was that large masses of peasants were evicted from their property and left landless and without sources of income. Those views were not based on observed evidence, but rather were assumed to be the case on the basis of merely theoretical social science models. It didn't hurt that New Testament academic scholars developed an ideological affinity for third-world Marxist revolutionary movements such as those led by Fidel Castro and then some of his protégés in the Sandinista regime in Nicaragua.

But since then, archeologists have done quite a bit of digging in northern Israel and what we see is a reasonably prosperous region. Sure, there was poverty, but not to the extent previously believed. For gigantic agricultural plantations patched together from the smaller farms of displaced farmers, Jesus would only need to stand on the Nazareth ridge and look away from His home province and down to the south. Digs, plus documentary evidence, show us that the picture that was attached to Galilee was more accurately applied to rival communities to the south.

Now let's look even closer than the region of Galilee, and zoom in on Jesus's hometown, Nazareth. It's an important part of the story, even a fulfillment of prophecy, as Joseph brings his family to settle there:

> But when he heard that Archelaus was reigning over Judea in place of his father Herod, he was afraid to go there. And being warned by God in a dream, he departed for the regions of Galilee,
>   and came and resided in a city called Nazareth, that what was spoken through the prophets might be fulfilled, "He shall be called a Nazarene."
>
> —MATTHEW 2:22-23

We know Nazareth was reasonably prosperous; not wealthy, but up-and-coming as an olive oil production center. Furthermore,

Nazareth was quite near to the cultural, political, and financial center of Galilee, a city named Sepphoris. This city has undergone extensive archeological exploration in recent decades and has been revealed to have been a city of remarkable sophistication, a thoroughly Jewish city, but possessing many of the benefits of Greek culture. It was quite prosperous, and both a bank and a theater have been uncovered, though it's not certain the theater was there during the time of Jesus.

It is almost inconceivable Jesus would have been unfamiliar with Sepphoris. When Herod the Great died, leaders of Sepphoris attempted to take advantage of the situation and revolted against Rome. The rebellion failed, and the city was destroyed. Then it was decided it should be rebuilt, and the rebuilding coincides with Jesus's teenage and young adult years. Joseph and Jesus were *tektons*, skilled builders specializing in wood. No major building project would go on without a *tekton*. They not only built structures out of wood but were also an important part of the stone work process in that they built frames to hold the stones in place and scaffolds for the stone workers.

Nazareth was a small village, and there were only so many yokes to build and doors to repair. Artisans like Joseph and Jesus made their living traveling near and far to work on large building projects. It would be highly unlikely they would not have worked on such a nearby, large, lucrative building boom.

Which means Jesus would have been exposed to high culture and to high finance. His financial parables show high levels of sophistication. They're not the sort of thing that reads like a peasant's guess about how investment processes operated; the numbers read true to life. Jesus knew His way around the world of finance, and now we understand the human agency by which He acquired that knowledge.

There is another very important point to make about Sepphoris and Nazareth: Sepphoris had wealthy people. Archeologists have dug up at least one expansive mansion. It's not as luxurious as the most ostentatious mansions in Jerusalem, but there clearly was a wealthy class right in Jesus's neighborhood. And yet we have absolutely no confrontations between Jesus and any wealthy individuals in His home district. He was willing to confront His fellow Nazarenes where appropriate, for example about their attitudes toward pagans. In fact, He was so confrontational that He was almost killed by His hometown. But the topic was not money.

Sepphoris was a trading center, but there are no records of confrontations with wealthy merchants, despite the fact that merchants were of a fairly prosperous class. Where are the confrontations with Sepphoris's bankers? Where are the confrontations with wealthy fishing merchants of Magdala? Jesus was aware of Magdala and dealt with the city; He even got a disciple from there, Mary Magdalene. That city was wealthy.

So was Tiberius. If Jesus was disapproving of wealth as such, then why do we only see confrontations over wealth when He was near Jerusalem and the ruling political class, but never see any such confrontations with those who became wealthy in the more entrepreneurial north? As we shall see, that pattern holds throughout the Gospels. The most reasonable explanation for this pattern of the Gospels not disapproving of honestly gotten wealth is Jesus doesn't disapprove of honestly gotten wealth.

But as Jesus moves south, closer to the capital region, He begins to encounter politically connected members of the ruling class.

Devourers of Widows' Houses: The Economic System of Jerusalem

We've looked carefully at the economic system of Jesus's home province (Galilee) and hometown (Nazareth) and nearby cities such as Sepphoris. We were able to see this region as a largely entrepreneurial society with broad ownership of property and reasonable prosperity based on farming, fishing, building, and manufacturing stone jars.

It had more autonomy than Judea and so was unlikely to have been required to pay taxes to the Roman empire. At least, we have no record in the Gospels or other contemporary sources about the payment of taxes to Rome. This means Galileans had fewer layers of taxation than Judeans.

This makes sense in light of the Gospel text in which members of the Judean ruling class, including Herodians, challenge Jesus about Roman taxes.

> And they sent some of the Pharisees and Herodians to Him, in order to trap Him in a statement. And they came and said to Him, "Teacher, we know that You are truthful, and defer to no one; for You are not partial to any, but teach the way of God in truth. Is it lawful to pay a poll-tax to Caesar, or not? Shall we pay, or shall we not pay?" But He, knowing their hypocrisy, said to them, "Why are you testing Me? Bring Me a denarius to look at." And they brought one. And He said to them, "Whose likeness and inscription is this?" And they said to Him, "Caesar's." And Jesus said to them, "Render to Caesar the things that are Caesar's, and to God the things that are God's." And they were amazed at Him.
>
> —Mark 12:13–17

There's quite a lot going on in this passage, more than we can deal with right now. For now, let's simply note what many commenters skip over: the very existence of the tax. Instead of skimming past that to "the main point," which is usually highly interpretive, let's stop and notice the basic facts. Jesus was in Judea. He was confronted by members of the ruling class about a tax paid to Rome, which means there was a tax due to Rome.

We also know this from other historical sources. For example, the Roman historian Tacitus said Judea was "exhausted" (*fessae*) by taxes and therefore appealed to Tiberius Caesar for relief. We also can see from this passage that the issue of paying "taxes to Caesar" was a huge controversy. If it was not a big deal, the passage would make no sense. Matthew says they wanted to "trap Him." What was the nature of the trap? If Jesus denied the validity of the tax, the Romans would seize Him, ending His ministry and His threat to the ruling class.

The other side of the dilemma was that if Jesus affirmed the tax, He would be risking His popularity with the crowds. This implies that the tax was deeply unpopular. Did religious leaders object because of the alleged idolatry of Caesar's image? Unlikely, because the official Judean currency also used images. The Jerusalem authorities had lost the privilege of minting currency and so Judean coinage was minted in Tyre, and it had images. So that leaves the most viable explanation for the unpopularity of the tax squarely on the issue of overtaxation. Judea was a high-tax, overtaxed jurisdiction.

That contrasts with Galilee. Perhaps the fact that Judea had this tax and Galilee did not is one of the reasons the rulers decided this was a vulnerable area in which to attack Jesus. Having a Galilean mindset, He would be more likely to reject the Roman tax.

There is also the issue of economic decentralization.

South of Galilee, on what is called "the Great Plain," economic and political power were much more highly concentrated. The Great Plain had some enormously large agricultural combines, parceled out to the politically connected. Some of Jesus's parables are reminiscent of large plantations like those. The Parable of the Talents, for example, shows an absentee landlord situation (Matthew 25:14-30). This suggests a very large farm.

Luke 16:1-12, the Parable of the Unfaithful Steward, involves rather large numbers:

> *And he summoned each one of his master's debtors, and he began saying to the first, "How much do you owe my master?"...And he said, "A hundred measures of oil." And he said to him, "Take your bill, and sit down quickly and write fifty."...Then he said to another, "And how much do you owe?" And he said, "A hundred measures of wheat." He said to him, "Take your bill, and write eighty."*

A hundred measures of oil—a hundred measures of wheat. A measure is almost ten gallons. These are pretty big numbers, large plantation numbers.

Several biblical passages describe what appear to be large farms with absentee owners:

The Parable of the Tenants, Mark 12:1–8; the Parable of the Workers, Matthew 20:1–15; the Parable of the Faithful Steward, Luke 12:42–43; the Parable of the Wheat and Tares, Matthew 13:24–30; and the Parable of the Prodigal Son, Luke 15:11–32.

By contrast, what Jesus would have encountered in and around Nazareth was freehold farmers—farmers who owned the land they worked and who worked the land they owned. Close to Nazareth, He would have met mostly olive farmers and, of course, people who ran olive presses to extract olive oil. Not far from there, Jesus would have met a wide variety of merchants in trading markets in Sepphoris, and given the fact that Jesus lived through two major building booms (Sepphoris and Tiberias) before He began His ministry, He would have had dealings with many small building businesses, like the one probably owned by Joseph and Himself. Both Joseph and Jesus are referred to as "carpenters," but the word translated that way implies a far broader set of responsibilities and involves a high level of skill and a fairly high level of income and social influence. More on that below.

In general, Galilee was a more equal society, a younger economy that had not—yet—reached the stratification and ossification that had turned Judea into a pit of manipulation, exploitation, and even enslavement. This would shock a young Galilean making a visit to the Jerusalem temple; shock and offend. If I am reading the Gospels correctly, a particular young Galilean was indeed offended by what He saw there.

Jesus's Galilean enmity against the Judeans sheds light on an ancient misunderstanding about the meaning of the Gospels. There are several passages that have been used to justify anti-Semitism. For example:

And for this reason the Jews were persecuting Jesus, because He was doing these things on the Sabbath.

—John 5:16

When therefore it was evening, on that day, the first day of the week, and when the doors were shut where the disciples were, for fear of the Jews, Jesus came and stood in their midst, and said to them, "Peace be with you."

—JOHN 20:19

The problem is that the word traditionally translated as "Jews" can just as easily be translated as "Judeans." The standard dictionaries include "Judean" as one of the standard meanings. The standard dictionaries typically include three definitions: a Jewish person, a Judean person, and a Jewish person who is hostile to Christianity. In my own reading, I noticed that the first definition is often used when Jewish people are being dealt with by non-Jews, for example Greek or Chaldean pagans. In the Greek translation of the Old Testament, the word tended to mean "Judean" before the exile broke down the distinction between the tribes and "Jewish person" during the exile. But what did it mean as used in the Gospels?

It probably meant Judean. First of all, as we have shown, the powerful enmity between Judeans and Galileans suggests a strong distinction. Second, the Gospels present a particular enmity between the Judean authorities and Jesus and His followers. As we've seen above, they used "Galilean" as a way to identify Jesus and His followers. It seems not at all far-fetched to believe the people who were casting aspersions on Jewish Galileans were not Jews but rather Judeans. Third, Jesus's followers were Jews too. It makes no semantic sense to say the Jews wanted to kill Jesus's followers, since both parties to the conflict were Jewish in religion and ethnicity.

Finally, translating the word as "Jews" leads to clearly nonsensical translations such as this:

And after these things Jesus was walking in Galilee; for He was unwilling to walk in Judea, because the Jews were seeking to kill Him. Now the feast of the Jews, the Feast of Booths, was at hand.

—JOHN 7:1–2

Why go to Jewish Galilee to avoid the general population of Jewish people? The word translated as "Jews" and the word for "Judea" are basically the same word. Why treat one as though it refers to a general ethnicity and the other as though it referred to a geographical subdivision?

A more sensible translation would be something like:

> And after these things Jesus was walking in Galilee; for He was unwilling to walk in Judea, because the Judeans were seeking to kill Him.

When the Judeans are trying to kill you, you leave Judea. Now that makes sense.

So, the thesis of this book is that Jesus's Galilean approach to economics placed Him at loggerheads with the Judean authorities, and them at loggerheads with Him. They oppressed their Jewish brothers and Jesus became a threat to that system of oppression, which is one of the things which made Him so popular. That's why the Judeans, or in other words the Jerusalem ruling class, were at enmity with Jesus and His followers. This both sheds light on the economics of the conflict and also helps to bury the far-too-ancient myth of an anti-Semitic New Testament.

Next, we will see how, from the very beginning, Jesus tailored His economic messages in ways appropriate for the different economic environments in which they were given.

Sermon on the Mount vs. Sermon on the Plain: Different Economic Messages for Different Audiences

If we know how different the economies of Galilee and Judea were, is there any question whether Jesus knew how different they were too? Some of the earliest pronouncements we see from Him in the Gospels show He did know and varied His message accordingly. For example, there are the accounts of what is called the Sermon on the Mount and the less well-known Sermon on the Plain.

45

These two accounts are often treated as parallel passages in separate sections of the Bible that describe the same underlying event but from somewhat different points of view.

The Sermon on the Mount and the Sermon on the Plain do not appear to be the same events.

They are sufficiently similar that critics of the Bible have cited the differences between them as alleged evidence of contradictions in the Scriptures. For example, they claim that because one account says the sermon was given on a flat plain and the other says it was given from a mountain, this means the writers of Luke's Gospel and Matthew's Gospel disagree with one another. The far simpler and more defensible answer is they were two different sermons given in two different places.

This lines up with the differences in the audiences. Luke's Sermon on the Plain is given to a largely Judean audience:

> *And he came down with them, and stood in the plain, and the company of his disciples, and a great multitude of people out of all Judaea and Jerusalem, and from the sea coast of Tyre and Sidon, which came to hear him, and to be healed of their diseases;...*
>
> —Luke 6:17 (KJV) (emphases mine)

Please note the presence of residents from Tyre and Sidon as well. The Judean elites and those of the trading centers of Tyre and Sidon had deep economic ties. Rome had diminished the power of the Herodians by removing authority to mint their own coins. The Jerusalem shekel was minted in Tyre. Officials from the New York Fed go to Washington to meet with government officials. This is kind of like that. Shamefully, these business ties included the slave trade in Jerusalem's open-air slave markets and the trading ports of Tyre and Sidon.

The Sermon on the Mount, on the other hand, had a different audience:

And Jesus was going about in all Galilee, teaching in their synagogues, and proclaiming the gospel of the kingdom, and healing every kind of disease and every kind of sickness among the people.

And the news about Him went out into all Syria; *and they brought to Him all who were ill, taken with various diseases and pains, demoniacs, epileptics, paralytics; and He healed them.*

And there followed him great multitudes of people from Galilee, and from Decapolis, and from Jerusalem, and from Judaea, and from beyond Jordan.

—MATTHEW 4:23–25 (emphases mine)

This audience was much broader and focused more in, or near, Galilee. First, it occurred after Jesus is identified as having been "going about in all Galilee." He was drawing audience from "all Syria," which is in the north near upper Galilee, and from Galilee and from Decapolis (which shared a border with Galilee). Judeans were listed as well, but the focus appears to be in the north near, or in, Galilee.

Not only does the variation between audiences help rebut the false notion that these passages are conflicting accounts of the same event, but even more importantly, it helps us understand the message of the passages at a much deeper level. It sheds tremendous light on the very different economic pronouncements in the two different sermons.

The different economic emphases appear very near to the beginning, starting with the first Beatitude:

Large crowds followed Him from Galilee and the Decapolis and Jerusalem and Judea and from beyond the Jordan. When Jesus saw the crowds, He went up on the mountain; and after He sat down, His disciples came to Him. He opened His mouth and began to teach them, saying,

"Blessed are the poor *in spirit, for theirs is the kingdom of heaven."*

—MATTHEW 4:25–5:3 (emphasis mine)

47

The Sermon on the Plain starts with:

And turning His gaze on His disciples, He began to say, "Blessed are
you who are poor, *for yours is the kingdom of God."*

—Luke 6:20 (emphasis mine)

See the difference? Poor versus poor in spirit. The latter, poor in spirit, is generally viewed as being less economically confrontational. It can be interpreted more broadly. One can be poor in spirit without being poor. One can be poor without being poor in spirit. Commentators who have wanted to turn Jesus into some kind of first-century Fidel Castro have tended to turn to Luke's Sermon on the Plain for ammunition. As we will see, they are right to see that passage as having an economic message, but wrong to see that economic message as a call to give the wielders of state power an even larger role in economic life.

So, the sermon given to the largely Judean audience focuses in an unambiguous way on the economically disadvantaged, who we will see below were the victims of economic exploitation by political elites.

Judeans and especially those from the capital, Jerusalem, are forced to sit through a speech from Jesus that offers blessings to the poor, off whose labor they lived.

But the differences go further than a blessing for the poor and include denunciations of the rich. Judeans get blasted with an even more in-their-face economic declaration:

"But woe to you who are rich, for you are receiving your comfort
in full.
    Woe to you who are well-fed now, for you shall be hungry. Woe to
you who laugh now, for you shall mourn and weep."

—Luke 6:24–25

But to whom is "you who are rich" directed? To the wealthy elite who ruled from the political capital of Israel, the Jerusalem political class and their favored interest groups, the rest of Judea, and their financial partners in Tyre and Sidon.

Please note Jesus uses the second person pronoun. He does not denounce the rich as an abstraction but rather "you rich," those to whom He is speaking, the Jerusalem ruling class, rich.

By way of contrast, the address given to the northern, Galilean-centric audience, entirely skips the section that calls the rich out directly. Instead it transitions directly from the Beatitudes to the affirmation, "you are the salt of the earth." In other words, in exactly the spot in Jesus's Judean address where He confronts the wealthy class, He substitutes a commendation to the salt of the earth.

Look at the non-Judean address below:

"Blessed are you when men cast insults at you, and persecute you, and say all kinds of evil against you falsely, on account of Me.

"Rejoice, and be glad, for your reward in heaven is great, for so they persecuted the prophets who were before you. [Omission of woes to the rich]

"You are the salt of the earth; but if the salt has become tasteless, how will it be made salty again? It is good for nothing anymore, except to be thrown out and trampled underfoot by men."

—MATTHEW 5:11–13

The variations between the addresses match perfectly with the different economic environments. You might have noticed it also matches the pattern we saw above in the economic comments of his mother, Mary.

It is very unlikely this is all mere coincidence. Jesus was a gifted and careful public speaker, the unique great communicator, and like any great speaker, He was knowledgeable about His audience and tailored His speech accordingly.

This will become even more undeniable as we see other examples in which Jesus carefully chooses His economic messages in accord with the nuances of different economic settings in which He speaks and the differing economic status of the people He confronts in His travels south to Jerusalem.

Were Israel's Rulers Allowed to Become Wealthy?

Before we dive into the details of Jesus's encounters with wealthy political leaders (especially the "rich, young ruler") and those connected with those leaders, let's first lay out what the Torah taught on the subject.

One of the earliest direct statements regarding the qualifications for political office comes immediately after the Exodus. The people no longer enslaved needed political leadership, and the burden of that leadership was far too great for Moses to manage alone. His father-in-law, Jethro of Midian, gave Moses wise advice, both about political delegation and about to whom political authority should be delegated.

> *Furthermore, you shall select out of all the people able men who fear God, men of truth, those who hate dishonest gain; and you shall place these over them, as leaders of thousands, of hundreds, of fifties and of tens. And let them judge the people at all times....*
>
> —Exodus 18:21–22 (emphasis mine)

Note the portion I emphasized, "those who hate dishonest gain."

Moses followed the advice, with a small modification. Instead of Moses choosing the leaders, he instructed the people of Israel to do so.

> *And I spoke to you at that time, saying, "I am not able to bear the burden of you alone....Choose wise and discerning and experienced men from your tribes, and I will appoint them as your heads."*
>
> —Deuteronomy 1:9, 13

The people were to choose political leaders who hated dishonest gain. Why? Because political office by its very nature tempts one to dishonest gain. It is such a powerful factor so singularly connected with the nature of politics that it is one of only three qualifications for public office listed by Jethro (Moses adds wisdom and discernment) and the only negative qualification mentioned. That is to say, it is the only character flaw that is singled out in the qualifications for political office, which suggests that, at least in the eyes of Jethro, it is the quintessential political temptation.

I recently learned from historian Daniel Dreisbach that this passage was invoked at a particularly crucial moment in American history, the Constitutional Convention:

> Convention delegates occasionally invoked the Bible in surprising and interesting ways. During debate on the qualifications for public office, the venerable Benjamin Franklin spoke in opposition to any proposal that, in his words, "tended to debase the spirit of the common people.... We should remember the character which the Scripture requires in Rulers."
>
> He invoked Jethro's advice to Moses regarding qualifications for prospective Israelite rulers, "that they should be men hating covetousness."[2]

Only lesser authorities are mentioned in this passage, not kings or other heads of state, but that is because Moses had already been chosen by God as the ruler and, therefore, no election of king or supreme judge selection was on the agenda at the time.

However, later, when the Torah does turn its attention to the choice of king, the issue of enrichment arises again.

> *When you enter the land which the LORD your God gives you, and you possess it and live in it, and you say, "I will set a king over me like all the nations who are around me,"...Moreover, he shall not multiply horses for himself, nor shall he cause the people to return to Egypt to multiply horses, since the LORD has said to you, "You shall never again return that way." Neither shall he multiply wives for himself, lest his heart turn away; nor shall he greatly increase silver and gold for himself.*

—DEUTERONOMY 17:14, 16–17

Even for the king, multiplication of riches while in office was not permissible. This was highly countercultural at the time, as royalty and great wealth were strongly associated with one another. If the king was not allowed to get rich in office, certainly subordinate authorities were not.

When Israel did choose a king, God warned them about the character of that king.

> *So Samuel spoke all the words of the LORD to the people who had asked of him a king....And he said, "This will be the procedure of the king who will reign over you:...he will take the best of your fields and your vineyards and your olive groves, and give them to his servants. And he will take a tenth of your seed and of your vineyards, and give to his officers and to his servants. He will take a tenth of your flocks, and you yourselves will become his servants."*
>
> —1 SAMUEL 8:10, 11, 15, 17

The warning is the king will take the wealth of the people for himself and also give it to his subordinate servants. That is exactly what was happening in Jesus's time, and it is exactly what we see Jesus confronting as He moves closer and closer to the king's capital. Herod engaged in numerous forms of forcible extraction of wealth from the people well above the levels authorized by the Torah or the needs of the national government. Herod then either withheld that wealth for himself or gave it to his loyal servant cronies, such as members of the Sanhedrin (the rich young ruler), and the holders of moneychanger monopolies at Herod's temple.

The warnings of 1 Samuel 8 perfectly anticipated the pattern of economic plunder, not just in Saul's time, but also in Herod's. It is with this context that we look at one of the king's servants, the rich young ruler.

Jesus and the Rich Young Senator

Jesus's confrontation with the rich young ruler is probably the most cited episode in the Gospels on the topic of wealth. Unfortunately, it is often cited by people who want to use it as a cudgel in their own ideological war against the market economy and in favor of centralizing more power in the state.

As I mentioned in the introduction to this book, years ago when I hosted a daily radio program, a leftist listener called my show and tried to use this passage from the Gospels to attack me for my free-market views. She quoted (actually misquoted) that passage as saying, "It is easier for a camel to go through the eye of a needle than for a rich man to go to heaven." That is a common misquote. The passage doesn't say anything about going to heaven. It mentions entering the kingdom of heaven, which is a different matter.

But aside from that quibble, the use of that passage as an ideological weapon in the leftist cause is a serious misreading of the passage. Jesus offered that statement as a commentary on a confrontation He had with a man of the state, a rich young *ruler*. Right off the bat, it seems quite unlikely Jesus intended His words to be used to grow the power of the state when the man He had just confronted lived off his access to the power of the state.

Let's take a closer look at the encounter:

> *And rising up, He went from there to the region of Judea....He was setting out on a journey, a man ran up to Him and knelt before Him, and began asking Him, "Good Teacher, what shall I do to inherit eternal life?"*

> —Mark 10:1, 17

Did you notice where this took place? It occurred almost immediately after Jesus entered Judea. Anyone who has read this far in the book will find it almost impossible to ignore the importance of this detail. Jesus (as well as Mary and, we'll see later, Jesus's brother—and

Mary's son—James) conforms with a clearly discernible pattern when it comes to offering economic commentary when in Judea, particularly in the environs of Jerusalem.

As I've said, Jesus does not confront wealthy individuals over their wealth while in His native Galilee (although He does confront His neighbors over other issues there). But as we see in this passage, almost immediately upon entering Judea, all that changes, and not coincidentally. This new tone toward the wealthy expressed while in the seat of political power is employed against a man who is explicitly revealed to be connected with that political power. Let's look at Luke's account:

> And a certain ruler questioned Him, saying, "Good Teacher, what shall I do to inherit eternal life?"
>
> —Luke 18:18

What does "ruler" mean in this context? The original Greek says *archon*, which is the word used to describe a member of a government council. In this particular instance, it implies he was a member of the Sanhedrin. The Sanhedrin was a center of political, religious, and economic power. Sanhedrin members were typically from wealthy and influential families, often priestly, and during Jesus's time, increasingly Pharisaical. Quite often seats were passed down through the generations, which explains a small and seemingly irrelevant detail of the text:

> The young man said to Him,...
>
> —Matthew 19:20

He was young and a Sanhedrin member, which points to his having inherited his father's seat on the council along with his land-based (we'll see that below) income stream.

Let's take a moment to look at the different emphases in the accounts of the three synoptic Gospels (synoptic refers to the three

Gospels—Matthew, Mark, and Luke as opposed to John) describing this event.

Mark's account does not tell us this man was a ruler. This is probably because that Gospel is considerably less lengthy with less room for detail. In addition, because Mark is almost certainly an early Gospel and written when the Christian movement was more Jewish, it would, consequently, be more Jewish itself. Which implies the man probably was recognizable and therefore needed no introduction. This fits with the fact that Matthew also does not mention the man is a ruler.

Matthew is undoubtedly initially aimed at a Jewish audience and so, once again, the man would be a recognizable social stereotype. This works in the converse case, in which Luke *does* mention the man was an *archon*. Luke was a Gentile, and his intended audience was also Gentile. They would be less familiar with the socioeconomic environment of Israel and less able to intuit that this man was a politically connected member of the ruling class; therefore, this audience would need to be explicitly told about his political office.

For more insight into the economic aspects of this encounter, let's take a closer look at the details of Mark's account:

>...And as He was setting out on a journey, a man ran up to Him and knelt before Him, and began asking Him, "Good Teacher, what shall I do to inherit eternal life?"
>
>And Jesus said to him, "Why do you call Me good? No one is good except God alone.
>
>"You know the commandments, 'Do not murder, Do not commit adultery, Do not steal, Do not bear false witness, Do not defraud, Honor your father and mother.'"
>
>And he said to Him, "Teacher, I have kept all these things from my youth up."
>
>And looking at him, Jesus felt a love for him, and said to him, "One thing you lack: go and sell all you possess, and give to the poor, and you shall have treasure in heaven; and come, follow Me."

But at these words his face fell, and he went away grieved, for he was one who owned much property.

And Jesus, looking around, said to His disciples, "How hard it will be for those who are wealthy to enter the kingdom of God!"

—MARK 10:17–23 (emphases mine)

Carefully notice the words and phrases that have been emphasized. Remember how I mentioned that the "enter the kingdom of God" phrasing is often misquoted? It is not "enter heaven"; it's "enter the kingdom of...."

Matthew's version used the Hebraism (remember I said Matthew was written for a Jewish audience) "kingdom of heaven," but Luke used the more universal "kingdom of God." What's the difference? You enter the Kingdom of Heaven/God when you repent and follow God and His heavenly ways. Entering the kingdom does not refer to the moment when you die. You enter heaven when you die.

In other words, this observation is about conversion, not the afterlife. It does not in any way imply a rich person who is a follower of Jesus will find it difficult to go to heaven when he dies. Moralists, leftists, and manipulative ecclesiastical money raisers should stop implying that it does.

Now let's take a closer look at the use of the word translated as "defraud." At first glance it appears to be a quote from the second half of the Ten Commandments. But when the reader pays closer attention, it becomes obvious this is a variation on the texts of the Ten Commandments. Defrauding is not mentioned in either version of the Decalogue.

This means Jesus added a commandment. Did He mess up His Bible memory verses? Probably not.

What makes more sense by far is He was making a point: This ruler, like most of the rest of the ruling class, was indeed defrauding. Whom were they defrauding? The poor, who were powerless and therefore ill-equipped to protect themselves from being defrauded.

That's why Jesus commands him to give his wealth to the poor: it was taken from the poor.

One might argue that defrauding was already forbidden by implication under both the commandment against theft and the commandment against bearing false witness. But that does not explain why Jesus quotes those commandments explicitly and then goes on to reiterate the principles of both against the specific practice of defrauding. This indicates Jesus put great importance specifically on the issue of fraud in the conversation with this particular man.

What reason would Jesus have to give defrauding such an important role with a member of this particular group?

Defrauding appears to have been quite common among members of that class.

The Greek word Jesus used is *aphustereo*. This is exactly the same word Jesus's brother James used (writing from Jerusalem) to describe the practice of the ruling class.

> *Come now, you rich, weep and howl for your miseries which are coming upon you.*
>
> *Your riches have rotted and your garments have become moth-eaten.*
>
> *Your gold and your silver have rusted; and their rust will be a witness against you and will consume your flesh like fire. It is in the last days that you have stored up your treasure!*
>
> *Behold, the pay of the laborers who mowed your fields, and which has been withheld by you, cries out against you; and the outcry of those who did the harvesting has reached the ears of the Lord of Sabaoth.*
>
> —JAMES 5:1–4

The phrase translated as "which has been withheld" is the same Greek word Jesus used, translated as "defrauding." The reason one word can translate into four words is that New Testament Greek

(Koine Greek) is an "inflected" language, which means it uses prefixes and suffixes to convey meaning.

Let me reiterate that the geographical pattern we've seen in the New Testament, beginning with Mary and continuing through Jesus and then even to His brother James, reveals that denunciations of wealth are correlated with proximity to Jerusalem, the capital of Judea. James was the Christian leader of the church in Jerusalem, so the geographical pattern holds even beyond the Gospels into this epistle.

Does James give us any help in discerning precisely how the rich ruling class defrauded the poor? Yes:

...Is it not the rich who oppress you and personally drag you into court?

—JAMES 2:6

As we see, the process of defrauding involves the use of corrupt civil magistrates. By the way, these magistrates often served on the Sanhedrin, the very council on which the rich young archon served.

In the Gospels, Jesus denounced lawyers for the sins of economic exploitation, among other things. James denounced the system that they had helped create by developing various tricks and work-arounds through which the Jerusalem elites could defraud the poor.

This is the type of defrauding to which both Jesus and His younger brother James referred, and both did it while confronting the Judean elites.

Interestingly, the word James used in verse 4, here translated as "fields," is *chora*, which quite often means "province." We will discuss that in greater depth later in the analysis of the Parable of the Rich Fool.

For now, readers should note the word James uses has more political than agricultural overtones. These elites were more likely "tax farmers," or those who managed other tax collectors. This fits with the more political/economic dimension we've seen so far.

The nobility used corrupt cronies in civil offices (such as those of the court system) and corruptible legal scholars to defraud the working poor who harvested their country. What we see is this was a system tied to the land, exploited by a landed gentry. That is exactly what the Gospel text implies about the rich young ruler.

> *And looking at him, Jesus felt a love for him, and said to him, "One thing you lack: go and sell all you possess, and give to the poor, and you shall have treasure in heaven; and come, follow Me."*
>
> *But at these words his face fell, and he went away grieved, for he was one who owned much property.*
>
> —Mark 10:21–22

The man was not just wealthy, he was propertied rich. That's implied by the use of the word "*ktema,*" which connotes real estate as opposed to financial property.

Once we understand the economic context of Jesus's confrontation with the rich young ruler, we're able to see a very practical dimension to His advice. Yes, the man idolized his position as a wealthy landed aristocrat and that stopped him from being a Jesus follower, which has potential eternal consequences, but let's also remember the city of Jerusalem stood under temporal doom as well.

Disaster was coming upon the land, with escalating cycles of oppression, rebellion, and violence, leading Jerusalem and much of Judea to be utterly destroyed. Being tied to the land made the rich young man, or his heirs, far less able to do the one thing that was most prudent for them to do to avoid the coming judgment: to leave. To leave behind a cultural and religious identity and also to leave behind doomed real estate.

Land was not something one dipped into and then out of. There were landed aristocrats, and there were merchants, and there was everyone else. The merchant class was somewhat suspect; the landed elites were an inherently conservative (in the sense of preserving the order at the time, not in terms of being committed to conservative principles such as free markets) class.

It's somewhat difficult for us to see the degree to which the land and the culture were intertwined. Think of the British aristocracy as portrayed in *Downton Abbey*. It's not just about the estate; along with the estate came a complex of spiritual and cultural attachments, or perhaps along with the cultural attachments came an estate. The Lord of Downton would almost have to have been loyal to the Church of England. The rich young ruler would almost certainly be loyal to the temple system as it stood and against the various reform movements.

There is another one of those subtle little details in Jesus's word choice that draws attention to the temple connection.

Jesus told the young man that if he sold the (landed) property (perhaps harvested by workers whom he then defrauded) he would be given "treasure" in heaven. The word translated as "treasure" is *thesauron*, which according to Nicholas Perrin in his excellent book on Jesus's conflict with the temple, *Jesus the Temple*,[3] usually refers to the treasure room at the temple. The *thesauron* was where not only temple assets were stored, but where the currency wealth of the elites was kept on deposit: two thousand talents (worth almost $1.1 billion in today's dollars.) That's right, the temple was also a bank and not only a bank, but a bank that played a key role in a system created by the legal scholars, administered by the temple elite, and used by wealthy elites to extract wealth from the poor. More on that below in the section on debt.

Jesus offered the man the opportunity to withdraw deposits from his treasure room at the temple in Jerusalem (slated for destruction) and to place them in the treasury room in the heavenly temple.

The Romans would sack the treasure rooms, raze the temple, seize the lands, and give them to those who helped Rome in its campaign. Those followers of Jesus who sold their property and severed their ties with the land were willing to flee when the end came.

Zacchaeus, the Tax Collector

Jesus continues toward Jerusalem after His encounter with the rich young ruler until He gets to Jericho and has another confrontation with a very similar man, who was also a wealthy ruler with whom He discussed fraud.

The details of the confrontation are provided by Luke:

> *And He entered and was passing* through Jericho.
>
> *And behold, there was a man called by the name of Zaccheus; and he was a chief tax-gatherer, and he was rich....*
>
> *And when Jesus came to the place, He looked up and said to him, "Zaccheus, hurry and come down, for today I must stay at your house."*
>
> *And when they saw it, they all began to grumble, saying, "He has gone to be the guest of a man who is a sinner."*
>
> *And Zaccheus stopped and said to the Lord, "Behold, Lord, half of my possessions I will give to the poor, and if I have defrauded anyone of anything, I will give back four times as much."*
>
> —LUKE 19:1, 2, 5, 7, 8 (emphasis mine)

Remember our interpretive rule for understanding the economic aspect of the Gospels: pay close attention to geography and occupation. Jesus confronts Zacchaeus on the way to Jerusalem. Look at the first verse above and notice "through Jericho." The Gospel writer makes a point of telling us Jesus is on His way somewhere else. Jericho is not His destination; it is part of His route to His true destination, which the Gospels (all of them) make clear is Jerusalem. But if it's a trip to Jerusalem with Jericho as a rest stop, why mention Jericho at all?

By now it should be clear we should ask what kind of economy Jericho had. Well, we don't know for sure, but there is a tradition that it was a favorite town of priests.

John Wesley, an English cleric and theologian who lived in the eighteenth century, said:

> From Jerusalem to Jericho—The road from Jerusalem to Jericho (about eighteen miles from it) lay through desert and rocky places:

so many robberies and murders were committed therein, that it was called the bloody way. Jericho was situated in the valley: hence the phrase of going down to it. About twelve thousand priests and Levites dwelt there, who all attended the service of the temple.[4]

It appears there was a conflict between Hyrcanus and Aristobulus, the appointed high priest, over Jericho. This may be the origin of the tradition that associates Jericho with the priesthood. This view is consistent with the Parable of the Good Samaritan, which occurs on the road between Jerusalem and Jericho and involves a priest and a Levite traveling on that road. This is, of course, not proof but is nevertheless highly suggestive.

We do, however, have proof about Zacchaeus's occupation—the Gospel specifies he was a "chief tax gatherer," that is, a chief over regular tax collectors. This makes Zacchaeus, just like the rich young ruler, a man of the state. He would probably have purchased (or perhaps have inherited) his tax farming monopoly.

People of this occupation were hated—so much so that rabbinical tradition forbade even sharing meals with them, and their gifts were not welcome in the temple treasury.

Financial corruption was quite commonplace, particularly defrauding the people by false accusation. This was used as a pretense to seize their property. The Greek word used to describe what Zacchaeus repented of, *sukophonteo*, is used on only one other occasion in the New Testament and that occasion also appears in Luke's Gospel—in John the Baptizer's commands to tax collectors and soldiers. That word is translated there as to "accuse anyone falsely":

And some tax-gatherers also came to be baptized, and they said to him, "Teacher, what shall we do?"

And he said to them, "Collect no more than what you have been ordered to."

And some soldiers were questioning him, saying, "And what about us, what shall we do?" And he said to them, "Do not take

money from anyone by force, or accuse anyone falsely, and be
content with your wages."

—LUKE 3:12-14

Why are these two occupations listed next to one another? What is the connection? This occurs for the simple reason that the two worked together. Tax collectors were agents of the Roman state, and therefore Rome's soldiers were the muscle behind the collection process.

John proscribed fraudulent overcollection by tax collectors. After that, it was to be expected their enforcers would want to know the implications for them. If their bosses were guilty, how about those who actually carried out the dirty work?

It is important to notice Jesus declared the salvation of Zacchaeus's house only after he offered four-fold restitution to the defrauded poor. Repentance was necessary, because Zacchaeus was guilty. He defrauded. That's why Zacchaeus knew which sin to repent of. Surely, he committed other sins—lust, pride, resentment, perhaps others. He only mentions fraud because that was the sin which characterized his occupation and determined his negative social standing. This is a highly defensible conclusion for the reasons given above and also based on how common the practice was. Add to that the fact that John's denunciation probably occurred in, or at least near, Zacchaeus's region of oversight.

Then Jerusalem was going out to him [John], and all Judea, and all the
district around the Jordan;...

—MATTHEW 3:5

In other words, it is quite likely that when John denounced fraud by tax collectors, it was those under Zacchaeus's authority.

Before we move on, let's say a bit more about Jericho. Biblical archeology can shed some light on the socioeconomic standing of this ancient city. David Fiensy, in his excellent book *Christian*

Origins and the Ancient Economy, presents some fascinating data about Jericho.

Looking at skeletal remains from a cemetery at Jericho, we find 39 percent of remains belonged to children. A comparison of remains from Meiron, a village in Upper Galilee, shows Meiron cemeteries with a 21 percent higher rate of minors. The average proportion of children that age in Greek graveyards is 26 percent more children.[5]

Child mortality is a bracing metric of comparative economic health and a heartbreaking one. Imagine the heartbreak and therefore the resentment of people in Upper Galilee, one of the poorer districts in Galilee, isolated in a mountainous region away from trade routes, who buried a fifth more of their children than did the priestly elite in Jericho. Of course, they didn't know the exact statistics, but the poor know when they're being exploited and by whom. The extractive elite, who lived in Jericho, literally were taking food out of the mouths of the rest of Israel via the Temple Tax and a dishonest system of currency exchange administered by the moneychangers. More on them below as we see Jesus passing "through Jericho" on His way to Jerusalem, the center of government power and of economic extraction.

Jesus vs. the Moneychangers' Currency Exchange Monopoly

Jesus's confrontation with the moneychangers has been used as political ammunition in an ideological war against the financial industry. For example, Franklin D. Roosevelt's inaugural address extensively referenced this text:

> Practices of the unscrupulous money changers stand indicted in the court of public opinion, rejected by the hearts and minds of men. True they have tried, but their efforts have been cast in the pattern of an outworn tradition. Faced by failure of credit they have proposed only the lending of more money. Stripped of the lure of profit by which to induce our people to follow their false

leadership, they have resorted to exhortations, pleading tearfully for restored confidence. They know only the rules of a generation of self-seekers. They have no vision, and when there is no vision the people perish.

The money changers have fled from their high seats in the temple of our civilization. We may now restore that temple to the ancient truths.[6]

Is this really a sound application of the event? Was Jesus really engaged in a general indictment of finance?

Not really. If you've read this far, you already know we have been tracing Jesus's progression (or is it regression?) from Galilee into Judea, escalating His confrontations in direct proportion to His proximity to Jerusalem, the center of political power. The denunciations of wealth correlate both with geographic proximity to Jerusalem and social proximity to the ruling class.

Jesus is tough on the rich in politically connected Judea and, when in Judea, toughest on the politically connected wealthy people: Those who are members of religious and political elites (typically the same people) who live off extracted wealth. Those who do not receive His verbal ire are those who created wealth through labor, commerce, or even investment. That last point—a tolerant attitude toward financial activity—was out of keeping with the culture in two ways.

The "conservative" aristocracy were land based and skeptical of the nascently forming financial markets.

David Fiensy makes this point very well in *Christian Origins and the Ancient Economy*. The ancient economy of the Mediterranean was overwhelmingly agrarian. It was based on land and farming. In such a system, more land, more wealth. There were very few options to deploy wealth but to buy land. One of the few alternatives was to invest in trading and shipping. But that was viewed as highly risky. Land, on the other hand, was viewed as the culturally acceptable and financially less risky investment.

But Jesus conspicuously goes against the grain on this point by telling a number of parables that involve finance, as opposed to agriculture, being placed in a positive light. Examples include the Parable of the Unfaithful Steward and the Parable of the Talents, as well as several smaller parables. And they all present a positive view of the investor character in the parable. Probably both of these parables put God in the investor role. Would Jesus talk this way if He thought of finance as an unrighteous profession?

Given Jesus's decision to break with conservative impulses in His culture and portray finance in a favorable light, it is unlikely His confrontation with the moneychangers was simply because He allegedly disapproved of the fact they dealt with finance. Given Jesus's criticism of the temple and its elites, it seems more likely their location on temple grounds was at least one part of His objection. The account specifies He confronted them when He entered the temple, therefore they were on temple grounds. He specifically criticized their presence there, contrasting it with Solomon's temple, which was to be "a house of prayer for all nations." Instead, it was turned into a "robbers' den"—a reference to Jeremiah, who also criticized the temple elites of his time. The text makes clear that this activity taking place on temple grounds was an issue.

> And they came to Jerusalem. And He entered the temple and began to cast out those who were buying and selling in the temple, and overturned the tables of the moneychangers and the seats of those who were selling doves;
>
> and He would not permit anyone to carry goods through the temple.
>
> And He began to teach and say to them, "Is it not written, 'My house shall be called a house of prayer for all the nations'? But you have made it a robbers' den."
>
> And the chief priests and the scribes heard this, and began seeking how to destroy Him; for they were afraid of Him, for all the multitude was astonished at His teaching.
>
> —Mark 11:15–18 (emphases mine)

And Jesus entered the temple and cast out all those who were buying and selling in the temple and overturned the tables of the money-changers and the seats of those who were selling doves.

And He said to them, "It is written, 'My house shall be called a house of prayer'; but you are making it a robbers' den. "

—MATTHEW 21:12–13 (emphases mine)

I've emphasized several phrases to draw attention to some points that might be missed otherwise. One of them, which I've already discussed, is the fact that the moneychangers were confronted after Jesus entered the temple, therefore they were on temple ground. Also, please note the phrase "robbers' den." I've already mentioned this is borrowed from Jeremiah. But it's important to see how appropriate this designation was. Jesus called this a robbers' den because they were robbers. The temple system was dishonest in numerous ways, which we can discuss in greater detail elsewhere.

One matter that stands out is the dishonest nature of the currency transactions. According to Alfred Edersheim's monumental tome, *The Temple*:

...But by far the largest sum was derived from the half-shekel of Temple tribute, which was incumbent on every male Israelite of age, including proselytes and even manumitted slaves. As the shekel of the sanctuary was double the ordinary, the half-shekel due to the Temple treasury amounted to about 1s. 4d. (two denarii or a didrachma). Hence, when Christ was challenged at Capernaum for this payment, He directed Peter to give the stater, or two didrachmas, for them both. This circumstance also enables us to fix the exact date of this event. For annually, on the 1st of Adar (the month before the Passover), proclamation was made throughout the country by messengers sent from Jerusalem of the approaching Temple tribute. On the 15th of Adar the money-changers opened stalls throughout the country to change the various coins, which Jewish residents at home or settlers abroad

67

might bring, into the ancient money of Israel. For custom had it that nothing but the regular half-shekel of the sanctuary could be received at the treasury. On the 25th of Adar business was only transacted within the precincts of Jerusalem and of the Temple, and after that date those who had refused to pay the impost could be proceeded against at law, and their goods distrained, the only exception being in favour of priests, and that 'for the sake of peace,' that is, lest their office should come in disrepute....[7]

So, the temple shekel was double weight, which no doubt had pious justifications about the glory—literally the heaviness—of the matters of God. But the bottom line is worshippers had to pay twice the amount, due to dishonest weights and measures. And the mechanics of this financial abuse were carried out by the money-changers. That is why Jesus calls them "robbers."

You may notice in the accounts of the confrontation, I emphasized phraseology that singles out the dove merchants as particular objects of Jesus's ire. Matthew's and Mark's Gospels mention the doves. Luke's account is generally similar but doesn't mention dove merchants.

John, however, focuses heavily on the dove sellers, so heavily that he portrays Jesus as speaking only to them.

> *And He made a scourge of cords, and drove them all out of the temple, with the sheep and the oxen; and He poured out the coins of the moneychangers, and overturned their tables;*
>
> and *to those who were selling the doves He said, "Take these things away; stop making My Father's house a house of merchandise."*

—JOHN 2:15–16 (emphasis mine)

What is the significance of the doves? Under the Torah, the sacrifice of doves was a provision for the poor. Poor people bought doves. The whole system of moneychanging was dishonest, but the dove sellers who charged double because of the dishonest shekel were specifically the group which was hurting the poor, such as were Joseph and Mary when they first started out.

> *And when the days for their purification according to the law of Moses were completed, they brought Him up to Jerusalem to present Him to the Lord*
>
> > *(as it is written in the Law of the Lord, "Every first-born male that opens the womb shall be called holy to the Lord"),*
> >
> > *and to offer a sacrifice according to what was said in the Law of the Lord, "A pair of turtledoves, or two young pigeons."*
>
> —LUKE 2:22–24

Luke doesn't mention doves, probably because his intended gentile audience would not understand this detail of Torah. But John has Jesus addressing only the dove sellers. Why would John be particularly focused on the dove merchants? Remember John was probably the closest to Mary who, as we saw above, was herself exploited by this particular group. Jesus arranged for Mary to adopt John at the cross and, according to early church historians, John and Mary stayed together, traveling to Ephesus.

This would also explain Jesus's anger. His own mother was exploited by this system. Jesus called out religious leaders for devouring widows' houses. Perhaps He thought of His own, probably widowed, mother. Jesus, on the other hand, was not a devourer, but rather was devoured by zeal for God and for the good of the people. That at least is how His disciples interpreted the confrontation with the dove merchants:

> *...and to those who were selling the doves He said, "Take these things away; stop making My Father's house a house of merchandise."*
>
> *His disciples remembered that it was written, "Zeal for Thy house will consume me."*
>
> —JOHN 2:16–17

But Jesus was not the only one who was consumed. It was immediately after this incident when the chief priests and the scribes decided to destroy Him.

> *And the scribes and chief priests heard it, and sought how they might destroy him: for they feared him, because all the people was astonished at his doctrine.*
>
> —MARK 11:18 (KJV)

They were consumed with fear at His popularity among the people. Up until then they were merely irked by Jesus because of His challenge to their religion, but now He was challenging their money, and for that, He had to be murdered.

The murder of Jesus did not involve the ruling class of Judea acting alone. They also used various pressure tactics against the Roman authorities (more on that later in the book) and, in addition, they had an "inside man" among Jesus's disciples. Given the pattern that has already been established in great detail throughout this book, you will probably not be surprised to learn there is substantial evidence this inside man had both ideological ties to the ruling elite and also geographically hailed from, you guessed it, Judea.

The Judas Economy

Everybody has an economic philosophy; economists are not the only ones who have economic views. This is true of Judas Iscariot as well, and in his case the Bible is not silent about his economics. We're told twice in the Gospels he was the keeper of the common purse. He complained about the gift of expensive perfume Mary of Bethany gave Jesus. He did not do this because he cared about the poor, but rather because he was a thief, and perfume was worth a large sum of money, which he would be able to pilfer if it were sold and entered the common purse.

He solicited a bribe from the chief priests to betray Jesus, a Jesus who we have already seen was under threat of death from those same chief priests because of His critique of their exploitative economic system. Judas took the money but then decided to return it. The priestly elite refused to accept the return of funds, so Judas "invested" the money in real estate in Jerusalem, in a field in which his dead body eventually ended up.

The story of Judas is economic all the way through.

But how did he think about economic matters? There is an overlooked detail that will help put all the information into context and out of which a coherent picture can emerge. We've talked a lot about how different from one another the economies of Galilee and Judea were. And we've shown how this difference goes back to the origin of Judea as a separate country and an economic exploiter of the north. And we've shown in great detail how much that division between Galilee and Judea sheds light on virtually everything Jesus says about money in the Gospels, from His early Sermon on the Plain to the final parable in Jerusalem that triggers the instigation of His assassination by the Judean elite.

The overlooked detail is that as far as we know, Judas was the only one of the twelve who was a Judean. Now, we don't know the origin of all twelve. We know quite a few came from Galilee as the stories of their recruitment are told in the Gospels. A few we don't know for sure, only by tradition. But we know where Judas was from because it was in his name and in his father's name. Iscariot is the English transliteration for two Hebrew words, "Ish," which means "man" and "Kerioth," which was a city in Judea. "Man of..." is the Hebrew idiom for city or country of origin in the Bible.

Judas, like his father, was from Kerioth, and Kerioth was in southern Judea. If you've read this far, you already know this revelation is not a pointless detail. It is a pointed observation. And to help emphasize this fact, Judas is the only one of the twelve who is repeatedly labeled by his point of origin. Eleven times Iscariot is mentioned in the Bible, ten times referring to Judas and once making a point in telling a story about another Judas who was not the same one. Interestingly, Judas's place of origin tends to be mentioned early in the Gospels, which gives readers a way of understanding his actions as they unfold. As if to emphasize this fact even more, Judas's place of origin is repeated quite often, not just mentioned once in the beginning.

His name, Judas, is also suggestive. The founder of the regime represented by the Herodian dynasty was a Judas. Judas Maccabeus led the revolt against the Seleucid Empire, which was part of the larger Greek empire, which was replaced by Rome as part of a succession of pagan empires that ruled the Holy Land. The revolt succeeded and established an independent monarchy in the Holy Land. The Herods seized control of that kingdom. So, to name one's child Judas at this time is at least suggestive of sympathies with that regime.

After the American Civil War, for decades after, freedmen took surnames such as Washington, Jefferson, Lincoln. Others named their sons Lee. Of course, people name their children for all types of reasons, often just because they like the sound of the name. But the Biblical tradition is quite different; names are chosen carefully and imbued with significance. When people hearing, or reading, these accounts at the time saw a disciple named Judas, it at least would have been quite recognizable, and suggestive. Of course, this proves nothing in and of itself, but as we'll see, the rest of the story strongly confirms what the name suggests, a heritage of sympathy for the Herodian ruling class.

Judas was very likely a Judean and somewhat likely from a family with an ideological affinity for the ruling political elite of Judea. Now that we understand that, we can see he functions not just as a stand-alone character, but rather as a stand-in for the Judean elite. Jesus's encounter with the Samaritan woman shed light not just on her, but on her group, welcoming Samaritans into the kingdom. Jesus's encounters with lepers and sinners and tax collectors were not just about those particular lepers and sinners and tax collectors, but about the groups of which they were members. Just so, Judas acts as a stand-in for the Judeans, with whom he conspires to have Jesus killed.

In many ways, his story perfectly exemplifies the Judean elite.

As we've already seen, the temple elite concentrated economic power into itself. One thing it did that is particularly relevant at this point is it "nationalized" the poor tithe. In the Old Testament law, the poor tithe was to be administered by the local elders at the gate.

At the end of every third year you shall bring out all the tithe of your produce in that year, and shall deposit it in your town.

—Deuteronomy 14:28

Only some of the tithe was to go to the temple, actually a small proportion. There is a lot of debate about this, which we don't need to clear up here in order to make our point, but the third-year tithe stayed local, and the other two years involved some going to Levites and some to the temple—typically this is seen as a tithe of a tithe going to the temple. And no civil penalties were attached to the tithe in the law. There were spiritual penalties, but no criminal penalties.

But what we know from Alfred Edersheim's *The Temple* and other scholars is the temple elite made the tithe mandatory, sending out enforcers with clubs to beat those who did not pay their tithes. In addition, the poor tithe was nationalized; that is, it was taken into the temple treasuries and administered centrally, allegedly for the benefit of the poor. Yes, the high priest and his cronies became, like Judas, the holders of "the money box," and they held it ostensibly for the good of the poor, but in reality, for their own good.

Judas perfectly encapsulates the Judean/Jerusalem elite economic philosophy: talk piously, engage in status one-upmanship, centralize control of money, and then plunder the money box for your own benefit. Here's the best example of that:

Mary therefore took a pound of very costly perfume of pure nard, and anointed the feet of Jesus, and wiped His feet with her hair; and the house was filled with the fragrance of the perfume. But Judas Iscariot, one of His disciples, who was intending to betray Him, said, "Why was this perfume not sold for three hundred denarii, and given to poor people?" *Now he said this,* not because he was concerned about the poor, *but because he was a* thief, and as he had the money box, *he used to pilfer what was put into it. Jesus therefore said, "Let her alone, in order that she may keep it for the day of My burial.* For the poor you always have with you, *but you do not always have Me."*

—JOHN 12:3–8 (emphases mine)

Judas plays the game well, using religious manipulation to get control of the money, something the temple elite mastered and for which Jesus condemned them (see the section of the "Widows Mite"). But Jesus plays a higher game, unmasking the whole thing in a powerful way. The command about the poor tithe (and its local administration) is at the very end of Deuteronomy 14. Immediately after that we get the commands about debt forgiveness for the poor. As you will see in the chapter on Jesus's debt warnings, "the poor you will always have with you" is not some maxim that Jesus pulled out of the air. He pulled it out of the Bible. Right after God told Israel to set the tithe apart one-third of the time to give to the poor in their own villages, God told them to forgive debts every seven years. Further, God told them if they obeyed His commands (poor tithe, debt remittance, and so on), there would be no poor in the land. But God goes on to tell them that because they would not obey:

For the poor will never cease to be in the land;...

—DEUTERONOMY 15:11

So Jesus is taking the conversation back to the Torah and reminding Judas the class he is a member of, or aspires to join, already stands condemned because if they had been obeying Torah, there would be no poor; certainly not enough as to stand as a highly visible image to use to goad people into giving in to a temple system that would not actually care for the poor.

Jesus's statement about the poor always being with "you"— meaning Israel's leaders, Judas's friends, not all humanity—unmasks the whole crooked system of monetary redistribution upward, accompanied by rhetoric about redistributing it downward.

It is interesting also this all occurs in Bethany, a site that was probably a city for the care of the poor. A defensible translation of Beth-ani, is "house of affliction" or "poor house." St. Jerome translated it that way, and there are early Syriac texts that indicate the same. Plus, the house of Simon the Leper is there, whose name indicates it is set aside for lepers. There were complex rules regarding proximity of lepers to the Holy City, Jerusalem, and Bethany meets those requirements.

Judas, who is stealing from the poor, complains about Jesus (who voluntarily left a prosperous occupation to live as an indigent) for allegedly not caring about the poor. And Judas, who is about to conspire with the temple elite, issues this complaint from a slum that would not even exist had the elite obeyed God.

Jesus saw all of that and exposed it with a short, paraphrased quote from the Torah: "the poor you will always have with you."

We know the rest of the story: Judas solicits a bribe from the chief priests, and they offer him thirty pieces of silver. Since the Bible declares this to be the fulfillment of prophecy, it is probably an allusion to thirty shekels referred to in Zachariah, though there are some questions about that. Judas takes the money, leads the temple guards to Jesus, identifies him, and collects his fee. He feels remorse and tries to return the money, but the chief priests refuse to take it, calling it "blood money," which is probably an allusion to some forgotten tradition that rendered money unclean based on its prior usage in something leading to a human death.

The money is used to buy Jerusalem real estate, turned into a graveyard to bury strangers, and it appears Judas ended up there. The thirty pieces were indeed blood money, but then that blood was sunk in the ground of Jerusalem, like Abel's, and cried out in condemnation against those who conspired against the Lord and against His Anointed.

As we will see, their escalating corruption and plunder and oppression of the poor would lead to the destruction of this elite. All Jerusalem would become a field of blood, which they would be buried in, strangers to the covenant.

To understand better why Jesus was murdered, we need to take a look not just at what He did, as we have been doing so far, but also what He taught, especially in His parables. A closer look at Jesus's parables will show Jesus was confronting the economic system of ancient Judea and those who exploited it far more often in the parables than has been commonly understood.

Once we've seen that, it will be far more understandable why the final trigger that set the plot in motion to kill Jesus was one of His parables, one that explicitly identified the extractive nature of the economic system and who specifically benefited. Jesus's early economic parables were intentionally somewhat difficult to understand, but as time went on, and as He geographically approached Jerusalem and the temple, His parables become more and more explicit and, finally, the elites fully understood that Jesus's stories were subversive to their economic interests. Once that happened, they decided to kill Him, and He stopped speaking in parables.

PART III

Jesus's Economic Parables

The Parable of the Ungrateful Nation

If you've read this far, you have seen over and over again how close, careful readings of the New Testament texts show us that Jesus was speaking with penetrating prophetic clarity about economic matters, often with barbs at the corruption of the ruling class. A close reading of the Parable of the Ungrateful Servant is another spot-on example.

First, let's look at the parable, with some key words emphasized for further attention:

> For this reason *the kingdom of heaven may be compared to a certain king who wished to settle accounts with his slaves.*
>
> *And when he had begun to settle them, there was brought to him one who owed him* ten thousand talents.
>
> *But since he did not have the means to repay, his lord commanded him to be sold, along with his wife and children and all that he had, and repayment to be made.*
>
> *The slave therefore falling down, prostrated himself before him, saying, "Have patience with me, and I will repay you everything."*
>
> *And the lord of that slave felt compassion and* released him *and forgave him the debt.*

> *But that slave went out and found one of his fellow slaves who owed him a hundred denarii; and he seized him and began to choke him, saying, "Pay back what you owe."*
>
> *So his fellow slave fell down and began to entreat him, saying, "Have patience with me and I will repay you."*
>
> *He was unwilling however, but went and threw him in prison until he should pay back what was owed.*
>
> *So when his fellow slaves saw what had happened, they were deeply grieved and came and reported to their lord all that had happened.*
>
> *Then summoning him, his lord said to him, "You wicked slave, I forgave you all that debt because you entreated me.*
>
> *"Should you not also have had mercy on your fellow slave, even as I had mercy on you?"*
>
> *And his lord, moved with anger, handed him over to the torturers until he should repay all that was owed him.*
>
> *So shall My heavenly Father also do to you, if each of you does not forgive his brother from your heart.*
>
> —MATTHEW 18:23–35 (emphases mine)

I emphasized "for this reason" so there can be no doubt this parable was told in a way that connected it with what came immediately before. What came before was Jesus's famous maxim about forgiving "seventy times seven":

> *Then Peter came and said to Him, "Lord, how often shall my brother sin against me and I forgive him? Up to seven times?"*
>
> *Jesus said to him, "I do not say to you, up to seven times, but up to seventy times seven."*
>
> —MATTHEW 18:21–22 (emphasis mine)

Have you ever heard that this phrase simply means "to forgive a lot?" I'd never heard anything else about it. But the problem is "seventy times seven" already had a clearly historically determined meaning, and that meaning was a matter of intense discussion right around the time of Jesus.

The Historical Context

When Judea was taken into captivity by the ancient empire Babylon (in the event known appropriately as the Babylonian Captivity), the prophet Jeremiah passed on a word from the Lord promising that after seventy years of servitude to Babylon, they would be returned to their homeland and Babylon would be punished.

And this whole land shall be a desolation and a horror, and these nations shall serve the king of Babylon seventy years.

Then it will be when seventy years are completed I will punish the king of Babylon and that nation, declares the LORD, for their iniquity, and the land of the Chaldeans; and I will make it an everlasting desolation.

—JEREMIAH 25:11-12

Later, the author of Chronicles explained that Israel was being punished for failing to follow the system of sabbatical years, which include debt remittance as well as a period of release from labor and of letting the land lie fallow.

And those who had escaped from the sword he carried away to Babylon; and they were servants to him and to his sons until the rule of the kingdom of Persia, to fulfill the word of the LORD by the mouth of Jeremiah, until the land had enjoyed its sabbaths. All the days of its desolation it kept sabbath until seventy years were complete.

—2 CHRONICLES 36:20-21

During the captivity, God, via the angel Gabriel, revealed to the prophet Daniel that even though the specifically Babylonian part of the captivity would last only seventy years, the time of waiting for full forgiveness and atonement would require seventy sevens of years.

Seventy weeks [literally seventy sevens, JB] have been decreed for your people and your holy city, to finish the transgression, to make an end of sin, to make atonement for iniquity, to bring in everlasting

righteousness, to seal up vision and prophecy, and to anoint the most
holy place.

—DANIEL 9:24 (emphasis mine)

Although there was a question about when exactly to start the clock, it was widely believed this period of 490 years was completed sometime during what we call the 1st Century. That's why there were so many false messiahs arising during that same period, as the Gospels mention on several occasions. Messianic expectation was in the air because the seventy sevens were almost over. And since the captivity was triggered by a failure to follow the system of sevens (and which therefore makes the punishment expressed in units of sevens appropriate), it was expected the new messianic era would involve the restoration of the sabbatical debt forgiveness.

Why was this so important? Because the sabbatical system was abrogated via a complex system of legalistic work-arounds shortly before Jesus's time. The Rabbi Hillel created an institution called "the Prosbul" that, while technically claiming to follow the Torah instructions about debt forgiveness, actually rendered it a dead letter. The way a Prosbul worked was a wealthy lender would sell his claim to a third party, usually the court, but there was a version in which he sold them to the temple.

The temple was deemed not to be covered by the debt forgiveness rules and could therefore continue to enforce payments. The original lender was thus able to retain the benefits of the loan beyond the seven-year limit. He would collect debt service payments for up to six years and then sell the claim to a third party with a value based on the loan payments continuing until the debt was fully discharged.

This puts the instruction to forgive "seventy times seven" in historical context. That number was in the air and in everyone's ears. And those ears would have perked up at its mention by Jesus (who by the time of that parable was seen as a clear candidate for Messiah/Debt Remitter). The fact the saying is immediately followed by a parable about debt and the parable is introduced with a "for this reason" transitional statement pretty much cements the case that the sabbatical year system of debt release was in view in the entire passage, including the parable itself.

Israel's elites were the ungrateful servants who, having been tentatively forgiven for not paying the King (God) what they owed Him—honoring the sabbatical year system as a condition of residency in the holy land—nevertheless turned around and sought to coerce every cent owed to them by the poor.

Understanding that this parable is about the debt-release laws, Israel's temporary reprieve by God despite violating those rules, their persistence in neglecting those laws by continuing to shake the poor for every last cent, and the judgment that fell upon them, helps solve one of the puzzles about this parable. Here's the issue:

> And when he had begun to settle them, there was brought to him one who owed him ten thousand talents.
>
> —MATTHEW 18:24 (emphasis mine)

The puzzle is the number is so astonishingly large. Jesus's financial parables feature numbers that are true to life; that is, they actually match the basic order of magnitude that Jesus would have seen among the freehold farmers and other small business owners He would have grown up around. But according to Biblical archeologist Dr. David Fiensy, the ten thousand talents mentioned in this parable were roughly ten times the annual revenues of Herod the Great, the king of ancient Israel. In other words, the scale of that number is much larger than business or personal finance size—it's of macroeconomic magnitude. And that's actually the point: it is a macroeconomic-scale number because it is describing a macroeconomic reality, a nation's accumulated debt.

If I tell you a story about someone who is $22 trillion in debt, then it is sensible to see this as an analogy (and parables are analogies) for a national debt. And it is likewise sensible, even without everything

I've already told you about the seventy sevens and the debt rules and all the rest, to see this as a story about the combined debt of a nation over several years.

The revenues of Herod Antipas, who ruled Jesus's home region, were 200 talents per year. Given the reasonable estimate of the standard 12 percent tax rate that Rome tolerated of its local kings, that implies an economic base of roughly 1,667 talents per year. Which makes 10,000 talents equal to about six years of economic output for the region. This number makes much more sense as a representative of the debts that would have been (should have been but were not) forgiven if the Shemitah laws were honored. That's one more piece of the puzzle falling into place.

Let's look at the final piece:

> *"Should you not also have had mercy on your fellow slave, even as I had mercy on you?"*
>
> *And his lord, moved with anger, handed him over to the torturers until he should repay all that was owed him.*
>
> —MATTHEW 18:33–34

Israel continued their disobedience by continuing to shake the poor for debts that should have been released under the Torah and, eventually, it became so bad political revolutionaries arose against the rulers, killed the high priest and his family, and then burned down the public records building in order to destroy the debt records, which stood as a claim against the poor.

Josephus surmises they did this in order to curry favor with the large population of debtors. This event inaugurated a series of events that led to the complete destruction of Jerusalem and the ruling class. The ungrateful servants who were forgiven so much for so long did indeed fall into the hands of the torturers, who tormented them into revealing where they hid their wealth, wealth they had shaken out of terrified poor debtors.

The Parable of Lazarus and the Rich Man

Is the Parable of Lazarus and the Rich Man aimed at the wealthy in general? That is how it was used during the Middle Ages when it was at peak popularity. This may have served a spiritual agenda with tendencies toward otherworldliness and deep ambivalence, at best, about the sacredness of nonclerical callings such as commerce.

But are such general interpretations the best ones? Up until modern times, texts in the original languages were either unavailable or difficult to find. The same was true of historical documents that could serve to put stories such as this in proper historical context, and Biblical archeology was nearly nonexistent. Now we have vast resources at our disposal, not just information that was not available before, but tools that help us analyze and access that information thousands of times more powerful than long form, hand-copied, inaccessible paper libraries in centuries past. So, of course, we should expect to learn new things, even about old books, like the Bible.

Let's look at this parable. I've emphasized some words I think will provide careful readers with important interpretive clues as to the original intended meaning.

The Parable

Now there was a certain rich man, and he habitually dressed in purple and fine linen, gaily living in splendor every day.

And a certain poor man named Lazarus was laid at his gate, covered with sores,

and longing to be fed with the crumbs which were falling from the rich man's table; besides, even the dogs were coming and licking his sores.

Now it came about that the poor man died and he was carried away by the angels to Abraham's bosom; and the rich man also died and was buried.

And in Hades he lifted up his eyes, being in torment, and saw Abraham far away, and Lazarus in his bosom.

And he cried out and said, "Father Abraham, have mercy on me, and send Lazarus, that he may dip the tip of his finger in water and cool off my tongue; for I am in agony in this flame."

But Abraham said, "Child, remember that during your life you received your good things, and likewise Lazarus bad things; but now he is being comforted here, and you are in agony.

"And besides all this, between us and you there is a great chasm fixed, in order that those who wish to come over from here to you may not be able, and that none may cross over from there to us."

And he said, "Then I beg you, Father, that you send him to my father's house—for I have five brothers—that he may warn them, lest they also come to this place of torment."

But Abraham said, "They have Moses and the Prophets; let them hear them."

But he said, "No, Father Abraham, but if someone goes to them from the dead, they will repent!"

But he said to him, "If they do not listen to Moses and the Prophets, neither will they be persuaded if someone rises from the dead."

—LUKE 16:19–17:1 (emphases mine)

The Context

Five verses before the story of Lazarus and the Rich Man, we see religious leaders being identified with greed and interpreting the story of the Unjust Steward as hostile to them. Greed and religious status are linked.

Now the Pharisees, who were lovers of money, *were listening to all* these things, [Parable of the Unjust Steward, JB] *and they were scoffing at Him.*

—LUKE 16:14 (emphases mine)

Interestingly the word used for "lovers of money" is virtually the same word used by Paul in his oft (mis)quoted maxim about the love of money:

> *For* the love of money *is a root of all sorts of evil, and some by longing for it have wandered away from the faith, and pierced themselves with many a pang.*

—1 TIMOTHY 6:10 (emphasis mine)

Now, let's get into some of the details of the story, focusing first on what "the rich man" wore:

Purple and Fine Linen

> *Now there was a certain* rich man, *and he habitually dressed in* purple and fine linen, *gaily* living in splendor *every day.*

—(VERSE 19) (emphases mine)

If purple and fine linen seem familiar to you, it might be because those exact words are used to describe what the high priest was to wear according to the Torah:

> *And these are the garments which they shall make: a breastpiece and an ephod and a robe and a tunic of checkered work, a turban and a sash, and they shall make holy garments for Aaron your brother and his sons, that he may minister as priest to Me.*
>
> *And they shall take the gold and the blue and the* purple *and the scarlet material and the* fine linen.
>
> *They shall also make the ephod of gold, of blue and* purple *and scarlet material and* fine *twisted linen,...*

—EXODUS 28:4-6 (emphases mine)

It's not just that the ideas are the same in English translation, it's actually that the same words were used. Of course, the Old Testament was written in Hebrew and the New Testament was written in Greek, so the way to match up the words is to look at the ancient Greek translation of the Old Testament made by a group of seventy rabbis (known as the Septuagint). This translation was popular in Jesus's time, and it is the version of the Bible used quite often when the New Testament quotes the Old. The words used to describe purple and fine linen in the Greek New Testament are exactly the same words used in the Greek translation of the Old Testament when describing the garments of the high priest. Listeners at the time would have noticed, especially given the extreme unpopularity of the high priest at the time and resentment against his, and his family's, opulent wealth.

And what is this man, clothed in an outfit matching the description of the high priest's garments, doing?

Feasted Joyfully

> Now there was a certain rich man, and he habitually dressed in purple and fine linen, *gaily* living in splendor *every day.*
>
> —(VERSE 19) (emphases mine)

He is "living in splendor," which is a highly interpretive translation. A more literal translation would be something like "rejoicing by lamp." Again comparing the Greek word used by Jesus with the Greek translation of the Old Testament, we see another parallel with the religious rituals of the temple.

> Now on the first day you shall take for yourselves the foliage of beautiful trees, palm branches and boughs of leafy trees and willows of the brook; and you shall rejoice *before the LORD your God for seven days.*
>
> —LEVITICUS 23:40 (emphasis mine)

Another example:

> But you shall seek the Lord at the place which the LORD your God shall choose from all your tribes, to establish His name there for His dwelling, and there you shall come.

> *And there you shall bring your burnt offerings, your sacrifices, your tithes, the contribution of your hand, your votive offerings, your free-will offerings, and the first-born of your herd and of your flock.*
>
> *There also you and your households shall eat before the LORD your God, and rejoice in all your undertakings in which the LORD your God has blessed you.*
>
> —DEUTERONOMY 12:5–7 (emphasis mine)

Even the New Testament uses the same word to describe religious rituals.

> *And at that time they made a calf and brought a sacrifice to the idol, and were* rejoicing *in the works of their hands.*
>
> —ACTS 7:41 (emphasis mine)

It appears this rich man is not only wearing clothes that match the description of the high priest's, he appears to be spending his time engaging in the same activities, "rejoicing" and doing it "by lamp." Remember, the temple had intricately designed lampstands.

What about the sole architectural detail we are given, the gate at which Lazarus is laid?

Gate or Portico/Vestibule?

> *And a certain poor man named* Lazarus *was laid at his gate, covered with sores...*
>
> —(VERSE 20) (emphasis mine)

The Greek word there is twice used elsewhere in the New Testament for the entryway to a temple. First to the temple itself:

> *Now Peter was sitting outside in the courtyard, and a certain servant-girl came to him and said, "You too were with Jesus the Galilean."*
>
> *But he denied it before them all, saying, "I do not know what you are talking about."*

And when he had gone out to the gateway, *another servant-girl saw him and said to those who were there, "This man was with Jesus of Nazareth."*

—MATTHEW 26:69–71 (emphasis mine)

And second to a pagan temple:

And the priest of Zeus, whose temple was just outside the city, brought oxen and garlands to the gates, *and wanted to offer sacrifice with the crowds.*

—ACTS 14:13 (emphasis mine)

So, the word used for the place where Lazarus, a sickly beggar, was laid matches the word used to describe the gate of the temple. This is especially noteworthy given that beggars frequented the general environs of the temple probably due to a belief that alms given near the temple were of greater religious credit and therefore more likely to be given.

My approach to evaluating interpretations is to favor those interpretations that explain the largest number of textual details, especially unusual details, and are not contradicted by any details of the text. Details such as the rich man's "five brothers."

Five Brothers

...for I have five brothers—that he may warn them, lest they also come to this place of torment.

—(VERSE 28) (emphasis mine)

Josephus tells us Ananus, the father-in-law of Caiaphas, the high priest at the time of Jesus, had five sons.

And now Caesar, upon hearing the death of Festus, sent Albinus into Judea, as procurator; but the king deprived Joseph of the high priesthood, and bestowed the succession to that dignity on the son of Ananus, who was also himself called Ananus.

Now the report goes, that this oldest Ananus proved a most fortunate man; for he had five sons who had all performed the office of a high priest to God, and who had himself enjoyed that dignity a long time formerly, which had never happened to any other of our high priests.[8]

—(emphases mine)

Ananus's five sons were Caiaphas's "five brothers."

Finally, the stories end the same way. A man named Lazarus rises from the dead and, nevertheless, neither were they persuaded.

If Someone Rises from the Dead

But he said to him, "If they do not listen to Moses and the Prophets, neither will they be persuaded if someone rises from the dead."

—(VERSE 31) (emphasis mine)

Jesus raised His friend, Lazarus, from the dead.

And when He had said these things, He cried out with a loud voice, "Lazarus, come forth."...

Many therefore...believed in Him.

But some of them went away to the Pharisees, and told them the things which Jesus had done.

Therefore the chief priests and the Pharisees convened a council, and were saying, "What are we doing? For this man is performing many signs.

"If we let Him go on like this, all men will believe in Him, and the Romans will come and take away both our place and our nation."

But a certain one of them, Caiaphas, *who was* high priest *that year, said to them, "You know nothing at all,*

"nor do you take into account that it is expedient for you that one man should die *for the people, and that the whole nation should not perish."*

—JOHN 11:43–50 (emphases mine)

And not only did they not repent, but they ratcheted up their evil in order to avoid having to change their way of life.

> *And it came about on the next day, that their rulers and elders and scribes were gathered together in Jerusalem;*
>
> *and Annas the high priest was there, and* Caiaphas *and John and Alexander, and all who were of high-priestly descent.*
>
> *And when they had placed them in the center, they began to inquire, "By what power, or in what name, have you done this?"*
>
> —Acts 4:5–7 (emphasis mine)

Jesus, the Messiah and true High Priest, did exactly what was expected of Him according to Messianic expectation: He confronted the economically corrupt, apostate high priest, who was almost universally seen by communities of Messianic expectation as wealthy at the expense of the poor, which indeed, he was.

Jesus's story would almost certainly have been interpreted that way by the people, given popular conceptions of the Messianic role, and since those are the people to whom Jesus delivered this message, that clearly appears to be its intended meaning.

The Parable That Got Jesus Killed

The parables of Jesus are not cute little stories designed to make His message clearer to the masses. How many sermons have you heard that say Jesus told stories because stories are easier to understand? That idea is nonsense, worse than wrong; it is the opposite of the truth. Jesus told parables so He would *not* be understood.

How do we know why Jesus told parables? Because His disciples asked him:

> *And the disciples came and said to Him, "Why do You speak to them in parables?"*
>
> —Matthew 13:10

Jesus's answer is (unlike His parables) anything but ambiguous:

And He answered and said to them, "To you it has been granted to know the mysteries of the kingdom of heaven, but to them it has not been granted.

"For whoever has, to him shall more be given, and he shall have an abundance; but whoever does not have, even what he has shall be taken away from him.

"Therefore I speak to them in parables; because while seeing they do not see, and while hearing they do not hear, nor do they understand.

"And in their case the prophecy of Isaiah is being fulfilled, which says, 'You will keep on hearing, but will not understand; And you will keep on seeing, but will not perceive;

'For the heart of this people has become dull, And with their ears they scarcely hear, And they have closed their eyes Lest they should see with their eyes, And hear with their ears, And understand with their heart and return, And I should heal them.'"

—Matthew 13:11-15

Does that mean Jesus did not want His parables to be understood by anyone, ever? No.

But blessed are your eyes, because they see; and your ears, because they hear.

For truly I say to you, that many prophets and righteous men desired to see what you see, and did not see it; and to hear what you hear, and did not hear it.

—Matthew 13:16-17

The Gospels make a point of telling us Jesus told parables in public but gave explanations to His disciples in private.

And with many such parables He was speaking the word to them as they were able to hear it;

and He did not speak to them without a parable; but He was explaining everything privately to His own disciples.

—Mark 4:33-34

Which raises a question about the Parable of the Vineyard, because in fact, the leaders did understand it. Here it is:

And He began to tell the people this parable: "A man planted a vineyard and rented it out to vine-growers, and went on a journey for a long time.

"And at the harvest time he sent a slave to the vine-growers, in order that they might give him some of the produce of the vineyard; but the vine-growers beat him and sent him away empty-handed.

"And he proceeded to send another slave; and they beat him also and treated him shamefully, and sent him away empty-handed.

"And he proceeded to send a third; and this one also they wounded and cast out.

"And the owner of the vineyard said, 'What shall I do? I will send my beloved son; perhaps they will respect him.'

"But when the vine-growers saw him, they reasoned with one another, saying, 'This is the heir; let us kill him that the inheritance may be ours.'

"And they threw him out of the vineyard and killed him. What, therefore, will the owner of the vineyard do to them?

"He will come and destroy these vine-growers and will give the vineyard to others." And when they heard it, they said, "May it never be!"

But He looked at them and said, "What then is this that is written, 'The stone which the builders rejected, This became the chief corner stone'?

"Everyone who falls on that stone will be broken to pieces; but on whomever it falls, it will scatter him like dust."

And the scribes and the chief priests tried to lay hands on Him that very hour, and they feared the people; for they understood that He spoke this parable against them.

And they watched Him, and sent spies who pretended to be righteous, in order that they might catch Him in some statement, so as to deliver Him up to the rule and the authority of the governor.

—LUKE 20:9–20 (emphases mine)

Note my emphasis above—*"they understood that He spoke this parable against them."*

This helps us understand why Jesus spoke in parables before this. Because after He told this parable, according to all three synoptic Gospels, He only told one more, a short one that is pretty easy to understand, and runs only one full verse, and is immediately followed by a prophecy about the destruction of Jerusalem. Why would Jesus spend His career telling stories deliberately designed to obscure their true meaning, but then toward the end of His earthly ministry tell a parable the meaning of which is so easily understandable it triggers plans for His assassination? After that, He stopped using parables to obscure His meaning.

Why?

Because the use of parables was designed to keep Jesus from being assassinated prematurely. When Jesus finally told a parable that needed no explanation (and please note that Jesus did not privately explain this one to His disciples—no need to), the immediate effect was for the temple elite to plot His murder. After that, the cat was out of the bag, and the period of parables was largely over; no need for obscurity anymore. Within a chapter, Jesus was denouncing the temple for its exploitation of the poor and predicting its destruction—one of the chief charges on the basis of which He was executed.

The fact that this parable so explicitly unmasks the economic motives of the Judean elites is an important part of the meaning of Jesus's crucifixion. In His early career, He confronted the theological problems of the Pharisees, and it certainly created backlash. But with this parable, Jesus was not just interfering with their theological problems, He was interfering with their money, and that got Him killed. He was killed for a number of reasons, but money was near the top of list. The Judean elite wanted to protect their money.

And it wasn't just the protection of Judean rulers at issue, it was also the protection of the Roman occupiers, whose own economic status was under attack. Not just the Judean economy, but the Roman economy as well played a role in the decision to execute Jesus.

PART IV

THE ECONOMICS BEHIND THE CRUCIFIXION

Is It Wrong to Talk about the Economic Interests Behind the Crucifixion?

We have already discussed the appropriateness of looking at economic and financial chains of cause and effect in the events of the Gospels. But now we are about to talk about what is arguably the most sacred moment of Jesus's most sacred life, His death. It seems appropriate to revisit the question of whether it is impious to consider economic causes when describing sacred events, so as not to trigger a mental backlash.

Why was Jesus nailed to the cross? Theology has tended to focus exclusively on the traditional doctrinal aspects of atonement theory, or on matters of personal piety or religious devotion. In this point of view, Jesus was crucified to save mankind from sin, to absorb our punishment, to save us. Those are matters of the purpose of divine intention and are, of course, of prime importance.

But God was not the only actor in this drama; there were many others, including the scribes and lawyers, the priests and the

Herodians, and then there were the occupying Romans—each group with different but interrelated intentions such as power, survival, and (yes) even money. The historical factors do not conflict with the theological factors. Just because the Gospels clearly indicate the ruling class at least partly wanted Jesus killed because He threatened their monetary interest, it does not in away obviate the fact that the Father, the Son, and the Holy Spirit had Their own reasons for what happened that day.

Yes, Jesus died because of our sins, but He also died because crosses cause asphyxiation and heart failure. When I've written about this or spoken about this in the past sometimes people have gotten the idea the one thing takes away from the other. Somehow, they think understanding money motives takes away from God's love for us or plays down our sins. But it seems to me that seeing how Rome's financial anxiety contributed to Pontius Pilate's decision to cave in to the mob and, in a major way, to the decision to give Jesus up to mob justice, contributes to our understanding of the nature of sin and forgiveness.

Let's look at the crucifixion through political and economic eyes. The Gospels unambiguously demonstrate that Pilate, the Roman governor of Judea and presiding judge over the trial of Jesus, tried to release Him.

Now at the feast the governor was accustomed to release for the multitude any one prisoner whom they wanted.

And they were holding at that time a notorious prisoner, called Barabbas.

When therefore they were gathered together, Pilate said to them, "Whom do you want me to release for you? Barabbas, or Jesus who is called Christ?"

For he knew that because of envy they had delivered Him up.

And while he was sitting on the judgment seat, his wife sent to him, saying, "Have nothing to do with that righteous Man; for last night I suffered greatly in a dream because of Him."

But the chief priests and the elders persuaded the multitudes to ask for Barabbas, and to put Jesus to death.

But the governor answered and said to them, "Which of the two do you want me to release for you?" And they said, "Barabbas."

Pilate said to them, "Then what shall I do with Jesus who is called Christ?" They all said, "Let Him be crucified!"

And he said, "Why, what evil has He done?" But they kept shouting all the more, saying, "Let Him be crucified!"

And when Pilate saw that he was accomplishing nothing, but rather that a riot was starting, he took water and washed his hands in front of the multitude, saying, "I am innocent of this Man's blood; see to that yourselves."

And all the people answered and said, "His blood be on us and on our children!"

Then he released Barabbas for them; but after having Jesus scourged, he delivered Him to be crucified.

—Matthew 27:15–26

Pilate's ruling that handed Jesus over for execution came after a rather lengthy negotiation with the gathered crowd. Pilate said he found nothing wrong in Jesus and was reluctant to have Jesus killed. But even beyond Jesus's innocence, Pilate had a far more selfish motivation than justice to want to let Jesus go. You see, his was not only a decision whether to release Jesus or not—it was a decision whether to release Jesus or to release Barabbas. Barabbas was a revolutionary brigand, an enemy of Rome. The New American Standard Bible calls him an "insurrectionist." That's anti-Rome stuff.

Now at the feast he used to release for them any one prisoner whom they requested.

And the man named Barabbas had been imprisoned with the insurrectionists who had committed murder in the insurrection.

—Mark 15:6–7

The Greek words used to describe Barabbas's insurrections are derivations of the word *stasis*, which is related to the word "state." Barabbas was a member of a movement that wanted to overturn the state established by Rome and governed directly by Pilate, the quisling state of the Judean elite. Matthew says Barabbas was "notorious."

We would say Barabbas was an infamous terrorist. He was an enemy of Rome and Pilate worked for Rome, which means Barabbas was Pilate's enemy and Pilate was his enemy. Pilate had every reason to crucify Barabbas instead of Jesus. Yet he spared Barabbas by killing Jesus. Pilate had two reasons to not want to kill Jesus, and one of them was tied directly to self-interest, so why did he end up doing what was against his interest, and killing Jesus?

It is inconceivable Pilate did this out of respect for the Jewish leadership. Pilate was not a kind governor. He was known for anti-Semitism: the Jewish thinker Philo of Alexandria believed he and Sejanus, who was Pilate's political sponsor, actually planned the eradication of the Jewish race, and Pilate was notorious for his harsh treatment of the Jewish people.

The early Christian historian Eusebius also records how Sejanus desired to destroy the Jewish nation and Pilate treated that nation very harshly, repeatedly doing things contrary to the Law.

So, the ancient sources show Pilate was a brutal oppressor, hostile to the Jewish people, and protégé of a would-be genocidal anti-Semite. And yet, somehow, he ended up capitulating to pressure from a people he neither loved nor respected and whom he previously delighted to humiliate. Why give in this time? The answer is in the details of Pilate in the Gospel texts:

> ...*Pilate made efforts to release Him [Jesus, ed.], but the Jews cried out, saying, "If you release this Man, you are no friend of Caesar; everyone who makes himself out to be a king opposes Caesar."*
>
> *When Pilate therefore heard these words, he brought Jesus out, and sat down on the judgment seat at a place called The Pavement, but in Hebrew, Gabbatha.*

Now it was the day of preparation for the Passover; it was about the sixth hour. And he said to the Jews, "Behold, your King!"
They therefore cried out, "Away with Him, away with Him, crucify Him!" Pilate said to them, "Shall I crucify your King?" The chief priests answered, "We have no king but Caesar."
So he then delivered Him to them to be crucified.

—John 19:12–16

The key to understanding the political dynamic of what is going on between Pilate and the mob whipped up by the Judean political elites is to focus on the phrase "friend of Caesar": in Latin, *Amicus Caesaris*. This is technical language referring to members of the Roman administration in good standing: counselors, senators, generals, and so forth.

With that in mind, it becomes clear the mob was threatening Pilate. The thinly veiled threat was they would write to Rome to label him as disloyal to the emperor. They had done something similar in the past, writing to complain to the emperor about Pilate:

But when he steadfastly refused this petition (for he was a man of a very inflexible disposition, and very merciless as well as very obstinate), they cried out: "Do not cause a sedition; do not make war upon us; do not destroy the peace which exists. The honor of the emperor is not identical with dishonor to the ancient laws; let it not be to you a pretense for heaping insult on our nation. Tiberius is not desirous that any of our laws or customs shall be destroyed. And if you yourself say that he is, show us either some command from him, or some letter, or something of the kind, that we, who have been sent to you as ambassadors, may cease to trouble you, and may address our supplications to your master."

But this last sentence exasperated him in the greatest possible degree, as he feared lest they might in reality go on an embassy to the emperor, and might impeach him with respect to other particulars of his government, in respect of his corruption, and his acts of insolence, and his rapine, and his habit of insulting people, and his cruelty, and his continual murders of people untried and uncondemned, and his never ending, and gratuitous, and most grievous inhumanity.[9]

That prior attempt partially worked. Pilate continued as a brutal dictator, though he did give in to the Jews and remove the cause of offense to them. Philo said Pilate did this in response to the command of the emperor, whereas Josephus said he relented in response to the entreaties of the people. Both agree he gave in. So, despite Pilate's and his patron's severe antipathy toward the Jewish people, the tactic seemed to have proven at least somewhat efficacious, which certainly tends to support the interpretation that they were going back to the previously effective strategy.

I don't want to overstate this. Pilate in no way became a gracious and merciful leader after this. He punished the Judean elite in a very effective way: he raided the temple treasury deposits, but in a politically manipulative manner, using the seized funds to build an aqueduct for the people of Jerusalem. A mob of Jerusalemites formed in response to this and violence spun out of control. Roman soldiers brutalized the crowds, and the sedition was put down.

> But they threw themselves upon the ground, and laid their necks bare, and said they would take their death very willingly, rather than the wisdom of their laws should be transgressed; upon which Pilate was deeply affected with their firm resolution to keep their laws inviolable, and presently commanded the images to be carried back from Jerusalem to Caesarea.

> But Pilate undertook to bring an aqueduct to Jerusalem, and did it with the sacred money, and took the water of the stream from the distance of twenty-five miles. However, the Jews were not pleased with what had been done about this water; and many ten thousands of the people got together, and made a clamour against him, and insisted that he should stop that design. Some of them, also, used reproaches, and abused the man, as crowds of such people usually do.

So he outfitted a great number of his soldiers in their clothes, who carried daggers under their garments, and sent them to a place where they might surround them. So he bade the Jews himself go away; but they boldly casting reproaches upon him, he gave the soldiers that signal which had been beforehand agreed on; who laid upon them much greater blows than Pilate had commanded them, and equally punished those who were tumultuous, and those who were not, nor did they spare them in the least; and since the people were unarmed, and were caught by men prepared for what they were about to do, there were a great number of them slain by this means, and others of them ran away wounded; and thus an end was put to this sedition.[10]

Judean elites learned that complaining to Caesar was effective but risky—which fits perfectly with the interpretation I am presenting. So why would they be willing to take that risk? The Judean elites were convinced that allowing Jesus to live would end up destroying the nation:

And one of them, Caiaphas, being high priest that year, said to them, "You know nothing at all, nor do you consider that it is expedient for us that one man should die for the people, and not that the whole nation should perish."

—JOHN 11:49-50

But why did it work so well that Pilate immediately gave in to the crowd, something completely out of character for him? The answer is economic in nature. Pilate was rendered politically vulnerable due to an economic crisis.

The Great Roman Financial Collapse of AD 33 and the Crucifixion

The following argument presupposes the reader holds to the traditional date for the crucifixion of Jesus, which I do. The general view of the church through most of its history, and the view held by many conservative scholars today, is that Jesus was killed in AD 33 (though a significant number of Bible-believing scholars are open to the possibility of an AD 31 crucifixion).

If the traditional date is correct, then a Roman financial crisis that began in AD 32 and crested in AD 33 could (and as you will shortly read, almost certainly did) play a role in it.

This financial crisis and the political fallout from it will help us see why Pilate would break from his normal pattern of dealing with Judean political pressure. It helps us deal with one of the great puzzles of the Gospel accounts: Why would Pilate, who hated the Jewish people, who answered to a man in Rome who hated them even more, give in to them?

The answer is there was, shortly before the crucifixion trial, a very serious shift in the political winds.

It is likely Pilate was appointed by his political ally, Sejanus, the Roman consul, second only to Tiberius Caesar. It was discovered in AD 31 that Sejanus was plotting an act of treason against the emperor. In other words, he was "no friend of Caesar." For this he was executed. Not only Sejanus, but his family, friends, and then many of his political allies were executed. His political allies were, like him, "equestrians," members of the same Roman class just below nobility, who were disproportionately found among members of the financial community. The crackdown on equestrian banking types helped trigger a very serious empire-wide financial crisis. Interestingly, this crisis seems to have originated in the region of Israel, specifically in the city of Tyre, where Jewish coinage was minted. Let me remind you that Jesus's denunciation of "you rich" in the Sermon on the Plain was directed against Judeans and Tyronians, who were closely linked financially.

Economic historian Otto Lightner, author of *A History of Business Depressions*, summarizes the ancient sources, Tacitus and Suetonius, and he is worth quoting at length:

The year 33 A. D. was full of events in the ancient world. It marked two disturbances as the outgrowth of the mob spirit. The first was in the remote province of Judea, where one Christus was tried before Pontius Pilate, was crucified, dead and buried. The other event was the great Roman panic which shook the empire from end to end. The consternation accompanying the latter died down and it was soon forgotten, but the murmurings of the former swept down the centuries until, bursting into flames, it enveloped the world. A description of the panic reads like one of our own times: The important firm of Seuthes & Son, of Alexandria, was facing difficulties because of the loss of three richly laden spice ships in a Red Sea storm, followed by a fall in the value of ostrich feathers and ivory. About the same time the great house of Malchus & Co., of Tyre, with branches at Antioch and Ephesus, suddenly became bankrupt as a result of a strike among their Phoenician work-men and the embezzlements of a freedman manager.... The Via Sacra was the Wall Street of Rome, and this thoroughfare was teeming with excited merchants. These two firms looked to other bankers for aid, the same as is done in modern days, but unfortunately at this time an outbreak had occurred among the semi-civilized people of North Gaul, where a great deal of Roman capital had been invested, and a moratorium had been declared by the government on account of the disturbed conditions. Other bankers, fearing the suspended conditions, refused to aid the first two houses and this augmented the crisis. Money was tight for another reason: agriculture had been on a decline for some years and Tiberius had proclaimed that one-third of every senator's fortune must be invested in lands within the province of Italy in order to recoup their agricultural production....[11]

Tiberius suddenly imposed such onerous local real estate regulation (an all-too-disturbingly familiar combination of two recent economic errors—subsidized real estate and trade protections) on the markets in order to punish the political allies of Sejanus. Almost immediately after Tiberius learned Sejanus was plotting a coup and killed him, his (Tiberius's) loyalists launched a wave of retribution against any who were associated with Sejanus. The financial community was close to the now-hated Sejanus, so they were subjected to these onerous government mandates. It is no surprise this triggered a severe financial collapse (much like burdensome politically motivated regulations helped to trigger our own financial crisis in 2008), driving the entire Roman Empire into panic.

The panic was fast spreading throughout all the province of Rome and the civilized world. News came of the failure of the great Corinthian bank, Leucippus' Sons, followed within a few days by a strong banking house in Carthage. By this time all the surviving banks on the Via Sacra had suspended payment to the depositors. Two banks in Lyons next were obliged to suspend; likewise, another in Byzantium. From all provincial towns creditors ran to bankers and debtors with cries of keen distress only to be met with an answer of failure or bankruptcy.

The legal rate of interest in Rome was then 12 per cent and this rose beyond bounds. The praetor's court was filled with creditors demanding the auctioning of the debtors' property and slaves; valuable villas were sold for trifles, and many men who were reputed to be rich and of large fortune were reduced to pauperism. This condition existed not only in Rome, but throughout the empire. Gracchus, the praetor, who saw the calamity threatening the very foundation of all the commerce and industry of the empire, dispatched a message to the emperor, Tiberius, in his villa at Capri. The merchants waited breathlessly for four days until the courier returned. The Senate assembled quickly while a vast throng, slaves and millionaires, elbow to elbow, waited in the forum outside for tidings of the emperor's action.[12]

Romans were panicked, but the financiers were terrified. This was the class allied with Sejanus, and they were also a part of a power bloc to which Pontius Pilate was tied. Sejanus, who was Pilate's political patron, had very recently been accused of the capital crime of being "no friend of Caesar, *non amicus Caesaris*," was found guilty and beheaded. Now Pilate himself was suddenly being accused of the same thing. Pilate's political cover was politically and financially bankrupt. Pilate's allies in the Equestrian Class were left with no financial capital and, as a result, no political capital either. In such an environment, the threat from the Judeans carried a much higher level of potency than it ever had before.

Given the new political realities, finances in chaos, Sejanus's friends on the outs, if the locals followed through on their threat that if Pilate released Jesus they would send a message to Tiberius charging Pilate of disloyalty, that message could come to a Caesar with a very different mindset than he had before, when a similar complaint was sent. Things would be different.

This charge would be evaluated by a Caesar who had just executed Pilate's political patron in Rome and who was pursuing a campaign of vengeance against that patron's network. This threat was addressed to a Pilate who also had a very different mindset, a man who was dominated by fear because his allies were reduced from financial masters to beggars. All this occurred at a moment of universal financial anxiety. Do you remember how things felt in 2008–2009? Add some beheadings and you get a sense of just how tense things were in AD 33.

So, the usually hard-line Roman cynic Pilate was much more easily pushed around, including being pushed into rubber-stamping the unjust execution of the peaceful Jesus of Nazareth and the release of the insurrectionist Barabbas.

People change during financial panics. Wars and also persecutions against minorities are more likely. People stop worrying about justice and start worrying about their own necks. For example, there is a historical correlation between inflation crises and witch burnings. Boom-and-bust cycles have far more powerful social consequences than economists typically see. The former Augustan building boom, which was financed through the Roman treasury, ended, and it was followed by a period of "austerity" under Tiberius and then a deflationary bust. The resulting increased social anxiety raised the risk perceptions of all elites, including Pontius Pilate.

It's not hard to grasp why the powers-that-be in Jerusalem would come to consensus on the murder of a popular grassroots leader who could show legitimate claims to the throne. Jesus was a threat to the legitimacy of the rule of the corrupt interest groups at the center of the Judean economy. He was genuinely exposing the machinations of wealth extractors such as tax collectors and moneychangers. Elites had a good thing going (for themselves, not for the nation). They could live off forcibly extracted wealth in the form of taxes, which included tithes recently taken on the force of law, making them a kind of religious tax.

Financial anxiety is an overpowering social and psychological force. It may seem strange to many people that financial anxiety was a serious factor in leading to the crucifixion; they're used to thinking about religion and economics in completely separated mental boxes. But to those of you who have read this far, it should not seem strange at all. You have seen over and over again how Jesus upended not just the tables of the moneychangers, but the whole corrupt system of state extraction of wealth on which those tables rested.

And you have already been shown the Jesus who warned in repeated parables and economic statements about the evil nature of the worship of money and power. Once you know that, it would be strange to not find extensive economic and financial forces at work in the events leading up to the cross.

The financial crisis that spread from the Middle East to the rest of the empire, and which helped trigger the crucifixion, ended when Rome embraced a bail-out strategy:

Tiberius was a wise ruler and solved the problem with his usual good sense. He suspended temporarily the processes of debt and distributed 100,000,000 sesterces from the imperial treasury to the solvent bankers to be loaned to needy debtors without interest for three years. Following this action the panic in Alexandria, Carthage and Corinth quieted.

Neither throwing Jesus to the mobs in Jerusalem nor flooding the Roman mobs with vast sums of easy money purchased permanent civil peace for either city.

The Roman bank bailout seemed to involve the establishment of Rome's first central bank, but far from stabilizing the system, easy money as a source of social pacification ended up acting as a mechanism of currency value destabilization. Archeological data show that shortly after this bailout, Roman currency underwent a series of debasements, and political crises occurred within a generation of the crisis and the crucifixion.

As for Jerusalem, as we've seen, the crucifixion was intended to protect the Judean economy and the elites who were able to manipulate it for their own benefit. They did it because the "council," that is, the Sanhedrin, was afraid of losing its advantageous situation.

Therefore the chief priests and the Pharisees convened a council, and were saying, "What are we doing? For this man is performing many signs.

"If we let Him go on like this, all men will believe in Him, and the Romans will come and take away both our place and our nation."

—JOHN 11:47–48

Their concern was twofold—the nation and their "place," their position, would be "taken away" (Greek, *airo*). Back at the beginning of Jesus's life, this was exactly what caused Herod to be troubled "and all Jerusalem with him," that their place and their nation would be taken away. They were right to fear it, but wrong to murder Jesus to avoid it. In fact, according to Jesus's Parable of the Vineyard (discussed above), it is precisely the killing of the true heir in an attempt to keep their place that triggered the judgment of the vineyard owner against the vineyard workers.

After Jesus tells the parable, He interprets it for, and applies it to, the Judean elites, the keepers of God's vineyard:

> *Therefore I say to you, the kingdom of God will be taken away from you, and be given to a nation producing the fruit of it.*
>
> —MATTHEW 21:43

When Jesus says "taken away" in this passage, He uses the same Greek word, *airo*, that the high priest used when he warned about their nation and their place being "taken away." They feared the Romans would "take away" their place, so they conspired against the heir and by so doing, triggered the thing they feared most: the taking away of their place. By putting their place above their relationship with God, they lost both their place and their relationship with God.

But they did not lose their nation and their place right away. As Jesus warned them, it would happen within "this generation." And the final trigger would be something Jesus warned them about repeatedly from the first announcement of His public ministry up until and including the day of His death. What did Jesus warn them against, which ultimately triggered their destruction? Debt. Next up we'll look at Jesus's debt warnings; how they were ignored, and how ignoring them caused the loss of the nation.

PART V

JESUS'S WARNINGS ABOUT DEBT AND DEATH

Debt Goes Back to the Very Beginning of History

How often did Jesus talk about debt? I've heard it said He spoke about debt very little. As we shall see below, that is certainly not the truth. But even before we delve into Jesus's statements about debt, we should probably consider whether He is likely to have spoken about debt. Jesus said the law and the prophets were about Him. If the Hebrew Bible talks about debt often and it is about Jesus, then it would be expected debt would be an important aspect of Jesus's life and teachings. Does the Old Testament talk about debt? Yes, it does, and it is not a rare or a tangential topic.

The Torah says a considerable amount about debt and debt forgiveness. Proverbs has many warnings about debt, and in the New Testament, Paul seems also to have at least discouraged debt; but by and large, debt is not considered an important part of Jesus's message, and that is a significant misunderstanding.

Not only did Jesus talk about debt, but it was a major theme for Him, not a side message. And we should expect debt to be one of the most important topics for Jesus, because it is an important part of the

Old Testament going back to the very beginning, all the way back to the Garden of Eden.

Beguiled and Indebted

After Adam and his bride ate from the Tree of the Knowledge of Good and Evil, God sought them out and asked them about the transgression:

> Then the LORD God said to the woman, "What is this you have done?" And the woman said, "The serpent deceived me, and I ate."
>
> —GENESIS 3:13 (emphasis mine)

I've researched this Hebrew text very carefully and wrote a 240-page master's-level thesis on the Hebrew text of Genesis, chapters 1–3. I discovered something fascinating about the Hebrew word usually translated as "deceived" or "beguiled."

Hebrew verbs are conjugated very differently from English ones. For example, they have grammatical markers that distinguish between situations where a particular verb is something the subject does and where the object is made or caused to do something. The particular word used to describe what the serpent does, depending on those grammatical markers, describes either the process by which one is deceived or, alternately, by which one is indebted.

The Holladay Lexicon defines the word when used in different conjugations:

> give one...*false hope...trick, deceive*....[13]

The *Brown-Driver-Briggs Hebrew and English* (BDB) *Lexicon* includes a definition, at least in certain conjugations, that focuses on debt/lending:

> "lend on interest, or usury, be a creditor" *also pointing to a cognate from the related language, Aramaic which means to "postpone, delay; sell on credit...."*[14] (emphases mine)

110

This is a bit advanced for a book of this nature, but try to bear with me. Biblical Hebrew has a set of conjugations, which is much more complicated than those we have in English. English has an active voice and a passive voice, but Hebrew has seven distinct categories that are overlaps of both active and passive voices, intensive and nonintensive, and causative and noncausative. The Hebrew word for what the woman said the serpent did to her often means to deceive and it is understandable translators would render it as "deceive" or "beguile," but in a different conjugation, it means "to indebt." Everything I just said was about the verb form, but in addition, the noun form of the word also refers to the act of indebting, per BDB lexicon:

[guile, dissimulation],...*lending on usury.*[15]

The words that are emphasized in the verses below are either the same word or the noun form based on the same root:

If you lend money to My people, to the poor among you, you are not to act as a creditor *to him; you shall not charge him interest.*

—Exodus 22:25

And this is the manner of remission: every creditor shall release what he has loaned *to his neighbor; he shall not exact it of his neighbor and his brother, because the LORD's remission has been proclaimed.*

—Deuteronomy 15:2

Woe to me, my mother, that you have borne me As a man of strife and a man of contention to all the land! I have neither lent, *nor have men* lent *money to me, Yet everyone curses me.*

—Jeremiah 15:10 (emphases mine)

Maybe you are not convinced that the word used in Genesis 3:13 has to mean "indebted" rather than "deceived." That's okay, neither am I. But I think that the evidence is overwhelming that there is a connotation that includes debt. Given that the word can mean either debt or deceit, related forms of the word often refer to debt, and throughout the rest of the Scriptures, the process of redemption from what happened in the garden is described in terms of paying a debt (in fact the very word "redemption" refers to such a transaction); the idea of completely excluding "debt" from the range of possible meaning here doesn't seem defensible. After all, the fact that the word and various related words derived from the same root can mean either "debt" or "deceit" shows us, in the thought world of Biblical Hebrew, that the ideas are closely linked.

But if what I say is true linguistically, that still leaves us asking whether this interpretation actually makes sense in the context of Genesis 3. Is there any sense in which the serpent indebted the woman? A full answer is very complicated and beyond the scope of this introductory book. In addition, the church has probably not given this question as much thought as it deserves, partly because theologians are seldom trained in economics and finance. You have already seen from this book so far how often there have been economic themes in the Gospels overlooked by most academic theologians.

But the denial of some sort of debt aspect to the fall is inconsistent with later biblical language about redemption: the idea of redemption automatically assumes a debt relationship. Words such as "redemption" have been read with religious ideas in mind for so long we have been conditioned to be immune to the obvious financial overtones of the word.

The same is true for "ransom." Ransoms are paid to buy people out of slavery, and slavery was quite often associated with unpaid debts. Are these ideas only metaphors? Only an extra-biblical disdain for financial ways of thinking would force us to believe that. Ideas such as indebtedness, redemption, and ransom are universal aspects of the human experience and part of our relationships with each other and with God.

The serpent promised the woman (who later is renamed Eve) that if she ate of the tree, she would be like God, knowing good and evil.

For God knows that in the day you eat from it your eyes will be opened, and you will be like God, knowing good and evil.

—GENESIS 3:5

That is exactly what happened.

When the woman saw that the tree was good for food, and that it was a delight to the eyes, and that the tree was desirable to make one wise, she took from its fruit and ate; and she gave also to her husband with her, and he ate.

Then the eyes of both of them were opened, and they knew that they were naked; and they sewed fig leaves together and made themselves loin coverings.

—GENESIS 3:6–7 (emphasis mine)

Their eyes were opened. The tree was desirable for wisdom. Eating from it did confer knowledge. Of course, it was all cursed. Like innumerable fairy tales of genies and devils, the devil keeps his bargain, but the bargainer always regrets getting what he was promised. But since the contract was kept, a debt was formed.

Paul affirms the same principle in Romans:

Do you not know that when you present yourselves to someone as slaves for obedience, you are slaves of the one whom you obey, either of sin resulting in death, or of obedience resulting in righteousness?

—ROMANS 6:16

Adam and his wife "presented" themselves to someone for obedience: Sin embodied, the serpent who crouches at the door of Cain wishing to master him as well as he mastered Cain's parents. Because Adam and his wife did so and obeyed him, the transaction is fulfilled in death. Look at the last verse of this discussion:

For the wages of sin is death, but the free gift of God is eternal life in Christ Jesus our Lord.

—ROMANS 6:23

I honestly am not sure who gets the wage: Is death the payment that comes to the first man and woman—what is due to them for their work of sinning? Or is death the payment the serpent gets in exchange for his work of helping them open their eyes and get knowledge of good and evil (from within evil)? Either way, there is a transactional relationship here. An exchange takes place after which obedience is promised and death is earned. This is core to the nature of the problem of humanity, which is why these ideas continue throughout the Bible.

Once you understand the interconnection between being beguiled and indebted in Genesis 3, a lot of the rest of the Torah falls into place. For example, the Old Testament presents a calendar with a system of debt forgiveness and property restoration in the Shemitah and Jubilee laws. These laws fit perfectly with the idea that the Fall in the garden involved indebtedness.

Adam and Eve were kicked out of the garden, a garden in which they could eat without cultivation (it was already a garden planted by God) and were indebted. They lost their home and their life of leisure and were made into debt slaves of sin. The Shemitah/Jubilee system inverted every one of those points. It returned Israelites to their homes, allowed them to rest from the labor of eating from the sweat of their brow, and released them from their debts. The Shemitah/Jubilee system ritualized the fact that eventually there would be a reversal of the effects of the tragic events of Eden.

In other words, if the Shemitah/Jubilee laws were a ritual undoing of the tragedy in the garden (and the reversal of exile from the ancestral home and the reversal of the curse of labor—even in only temporary ceremonial form), then the fact that these laws contain a debt-release provision implies indebtedness is part of what happened there in the garden at the dawn of history.

We will see below that though these debt themes begin in the Torah, they do not end there. In fact, they are picked up and magnified in the prophets and find their ultimate climax in the Gospels.

Torah and Debt Release

Remember, Jesus was a Jew, which meant He respected Torah, the "law of Moses." He quoted it extensively. He explicitly said He had not come to abolish it. He observed it (though He did not always observe the traditions that grew up around it), and He answered to the title "Rabbi."

So, if we want to understand Jesus's teachings about debt, we would be wise to familiarize ourselves with what the Torah teaches about it, and it teaches quite a lot. And we would also expect Jesus's teachings about debt to be influenced by and refer back to the Torah on debt matters. We shall see further on that sometimes Jesus says some things that sound a bit mysterious to us about debt, and that have been spiritualized away by our Christian traditions, but that come to make much more sense when viewed in the light of Old Testament teachings about debt.

When we find things like that in the Gospels, we should be prepared and even inclined to interpret Jesus's words in light of Old Testament teachings about debt-release over hyperspiritualized interpretations that deny any economic dimension to Jesus's teaching. In other words, we should take the Gospel at its word: Jesus was a Rabbi, which made Him an expert in Torah.

With that in mind, let's take a closer look at what the Torah said about debt remittance.

At the end of every seven years you shall grant a remission of debts.

And this is the manner of remission: every creditor *shall release what he has loaned to his neighbor; he shall not exact it of his neighbor and his brother, because the LORD's remission has been proclaimed.*

From a foreigner you may exact it, but your hand shall release whatever of yours is with your brother.

However, there shall be no poor among you, since the LORD will surely bless you *in the land which the LORD your God is giving you as an inheritance to possess,*

if only you listen obediently *to the voice of the LORD your God,
to observe carefully all this commandment which I am commanding
you today.*

*For the LORD your God shall bless you as He has promised you,
and you will lend to many nations, but you will not borrow; and you
will rule over many nations, but they will not rule over you.*

*If there is a poor man with you, one of your brothers, in any of your
towns in your land which the LORD your God is giving you, you shall
not harden your heart, nor close your hand from your poor brother;*

*but you shall freely open your hand to him, and shall generously
lend him sufficient for his need in whatever he lacks.*

*Beware, lest there is a base thought in your heart, saying, "The
seventh year, the year of remission, is near," and your eye is hostile
toward your poor brother, and you give him nothing; then he may cry
to the LORD against you, and it will be a sin in you.*

*You shall generously give to him, and your heart shall not be
grieved when you give to him, because for this thing the LORD your
God will bless you in all your work and in all your undertakings.*

*For the poor will never cease to be in the land; therefore I
command you, saying, "You shall freely open your hand to your
brother, to your needy and poor in your land."*

—DEUTERONOMY 15:1–11 (emphases mine)

The word "creditor," which I emphasized above, is a translation of
the same word-root as the word used in Genesis 3, discussed in the
previous chapter. In other words, in Hebrew the word for a "creditor"
is a very similar word for what the serpent did to the woman, which is
usually translated as something like "deceived." Again, we see that the
idea of deceiving and the idea of indebting are linguistically related,
and this creates a continuity between the garden and the Torah (and
later, the Gospels).

I've also emphasized an apparent contradiction in the passage,
which really turns out to be a paradox in the passage. God said there

will no longer be poor in Israel, but then shortly after that, He says that there will always be poor among the people of Israel. How can both statements be true?

These statements do not amount to a contradiction because they are both in the form of conditionals. IF Israel obeys, there will be no poor. But because God knows they will not obey, He predicts the poor will always be with them. And this should remind us of Jesus's allusion to this passage in Matthew 26, "The poor you shall always have with you," which we have already examined at length in the discussion of Judas Iscariot.

Let's take a look at Leviticus 25, which is a parallel passage:

> *The LORD then spoke to Moses at Mount Sinai, saying,*
>
> *Speak to the sons of Israel, and say to them, "When you come into the land which I shall give you, then the land shall have a sabbath to the LORD.*
>
> *"Six years you shall sow your field, and six years you shall prune your vineyard and gather in its crop,*
>
> *but during the seventh year the land shall have a sabbath rest, a sabbath to the LORD; you shall not sow your field nor prune your vineyard.*
>
> *"Your harvest's aftergrowth you shall not reap, and your grapes of untrimmed vines you shall not gather; the land shall have a sabbatical year.*
>
> *"And all of you shall have the sabbath products of the land for food; yourself, and your male and female slaves, and your hired man and your foreign resident, those who live as aliens with you.*
>
> *"Even your cattle and the animals that are in your land shall have all its crops to eat.*
>
> *"You are also to count off seven sabbaths of years for yourself, seven times seven years, so that you have the time of the seven sabbaths of years, namely, forty-nine years.*

117

"You shall then sound a ram's horn *abroad on the tenth day of the seventh month; on the day of* atonement *you shall sound a horn all through your land.*

"You shall thus consecrate the fiftieth year and proclaim a release through the land to all its inhabitants. It shall be a jubilee for you, and each of you shall return to his own property, *and each of you shall return to his family.*

"You shall have the fiftieth year as a jubilee; you shall not sow, nor reap its aftergrowth, nor gather in from its untrimmed vines.

"For it is a jubilee; it shall be holy to you. You shall eat its crops out of the field.

"On this year of jubilee each of you shall return to his own property....

"Do not take usurious interest *from him, but revere your God, that your countryman may live with you.*

"You shall not give him your silver at interest, *nor your food for gain.*

—Leviticus 25:1–13, 36–37 (emphases mine)

Notice how Leviticus places such a strong emphasis on sevens and sabbaths (which are extremely similar words in Hebrew). This system of sets of seven years and of seven seven weeks of years is very important: it is strongly associated with both debt (verse 37) and atonement and then later to return home from exile.

This theme, as you shall shortly see, is both assumed by and expanded in the prophets.

The Prophet Daniel on Debt and Exile

It was the prophet Jeremiah who clearly predicted the Babylonian captivity and who associated it with the number seven.

"And this whole land shall be a desolation and a horror, and these nations shall serve the king of Babylon *seventy years.*

"Then it will be when seventy years are completed I will punish the king of Babylon and that nation," declares the LORD, "for their iniquity, and the land of the Chaldeans; and I will make it an everlasting desolation."

—JEREMIAH 25:11–12 (emphasis mine)

Chronicles refers back to these words and makes more explicit what is somewhat more subtle in the original prophecy: the fact that these references to sevens are made in connection with the Shemitah system from the Torah.

Therefore He brought up against them the king of the Chaldeans...

And those who had escaped from the sword he carried away to Babylon; and they were servants to him and to his sons until the rule of the kingdom of Persia, to fulfill the word of the LORD by the mouth of Jeremiah, until the land had enjoyed its sabbaths. All the days of its desolation it kept sabbath until seventy years were complete.

—2 CHRONICLES 36:17, 20–21 (emphases mine)

Daniel extends this idea even further:

The prophet Daniel lived in the exile situation Jeremiah predicted. God revealed to him the period of exile would not be just seven, but seventy times seven.

In the first year of Darius the son of Ahasuerus, of Median descent, who was made king over the kingdom of the Chaldeans

in the first year of his reign, I, Daniel, observed in the books the number of the years which was revealed as the word of the LORD to Jeremiah the prophet for the completion of the desolations of Jerusalem, namely, seventy years....

Seventy weeks have been decreed for your people and your holy city, to finish the transgression, to make an end of sin, to make atonement for iniquity, to bring in everlasting righteousness, to seal up vision and prophecy, and to anoint the most holy place....

—DANIEL 9:1–2, 24 (emphases mine)

In the Hebrew, the two words translated "seventy weeks" are almost exactly the same word. In other words, "weeks" is "seven." Literally, this is "seventy sevens." This puts Jesus's statement to Peter about forgiving "seventy times seven" in a new light (or actually in a very old light).

The prophet Isaiah takes this theme, release of debt captives, a Jubilee theme, and associates it with the coming Messiah.

> *The Spirit of the Lord God is upon me,*
> *Because the LORD has anointed me*
> *To bring good news to the afflicted;*
> *He has sent me to bind up the brokenhearted,*
> *To proclaim liberty to captives,*
> *And freedom to prisoners;*
> *To proclaim the favorable year of the LORD,*
> *And the day of vengeance of our God;*
> *To comfort all who mourn,*
> *To grant those who mourn in Zion,*
> *Giving them a garland instead of ashes,*
> *The oil of gladness instead of mourning*
> *The mantle of praise instead of a spirit of fainting.*
> *So they will be called oaks of righteousness,*
> *The planting of the Lord, that He may be glorified.*

—Isaiah 61:1–3 (emphases mine)

Note how the liberty of captives harkens back to Leviticus, thereby aligning debt forgiveness, end of exile, and the Messiah:

> *And if a countryman of yours becomes so poor with regard to you that he sells himself to you, you shall not subject him to a slave's service.*
> *He shall be with you as a hired man, as if he were a sojourner; he shall serve with you until the year of jubilee.*
> *He shall then go out from you, he and his sons with him, and shall go back to his family, that he may return to the property of his forefathers.*

—Leviticus 25:39–41 (emphases mine)

The Temple Elite vs. Debtors

As you saw above, Israel was sent into exile because it failed to follow the Sabbath year laws. Did the ruling class of Israel learn from the punishment? After God offered a tentative relief of Israel's punishment, the people were sent back to Israel because there was a kind of forgiveness of their debt; that is, their obligation to God to obey these rules. But did they turn around and forgive their debtors? No, they did not. Just like the Ungrateful Servant in the parable, the ruling class had their debt forgiven, but they did not forgive the debts of the people.

According to Talmudic scholar Alfred Edersheim in his extremely detailed and well-documented book *The Temple*, shortly before the time of Jesus, the scribes and lawyers created a loophole that allowed them to work around the debt release laws:

Rabbi Hillel...devised a formula called "prosbul" (probably "addition," from a Greek word to the same effect), by which the rights of a *creditor were fully secured.* The "Prosbul," ran thus: "I, A. B., hand to you, the judges of C. D. (a declaration), to the effect that I may claim any debt due to me at whatever time I please." This "Prosbul," signed by the judges or by witnesses, enabled a *creditor to claim money lent even in the sabbatical year,* (Mish Shev, sct x.) and though professedly applying only to debts on real property, was so worded as to cover every case.[16] (emphases mine)

Nicholas Perrin, in *Jesus the Temple*, sees the same thing:

According to the Mishnah (Sheb. 10:3) the prosbul was enacted by Hillel (first century BCE) to counter the provision in the Torah for cancellation of debts every seven years (Deuteronomy 15:1-18; also Exodus 21:2-6; 23:10-11; Leviticus 25:2-7). It was a legal fiction that *assigned the loan to the court to collect a debt...* ("A prosbul-loan is not cancelled [by the seventh year]" (m. Sheb. 10:3)...[17] (emphasis mine)

The point is also made and further documented by Professor David Fiensy in his groundbreaking book *Christian Origins and the Ancient Economy*:

> The papyrus text from Wadi Muraba'at...dating from the year 56 CE, may illustrate the application of the prosbul. Goodman maintains that the prosbul would have been necessary only for rich people lending to poor ones. Rich persons lending to other rich persons could count on repayment because of the pressures of *social stigma* and thus would not need special legislation. Goodman assumes that many peasants would have been unable to repay the loans and thus would have faced *foreclosure* on their farms.[18]

> —(emphases mine)

Everything I've written above presents a rich background against which to understand the teachings of Jesus that pertain to debt and debt forgiveness and the consequences of neglecting the latter.

In this context, let us look then at Jesus's first public pronouncements about His calling, which He explicitly sees as a fulfillment of the prophetic promise of the coming Jubilee:

> *And the book of the prophet Isaiah was handed to Him. And He opened the book, and found the place where it was written,*
>
> *"The Spirit of the Lord is upon Me, Because He anointed Me to preach the gospel to the poor. He has sent Me to proclaim release to the captives, And recovery of sight to the blind, To set free those who are downtrodden,*
>
> *To proclaim the favorable year of the Lord."*
>
> *And He closed the book, and gave it back to the attendant, and sat down; and the eyes of all in the synagogue were fixed upon Him.*
>
> *And He began to say to them, "Today this Scripture has been fulfilled in your hearing."*

> —LUKE 4:17–21 (emphasis mine)

Let's give the most pertinent part of this announcement the proper emphasis. Jesus could have started His ministry on many other Messianic themes—but He decided to start it with Isaiah's announcement that Israel would be released from exile and from debt in accordance with the Torah.

This would not have surprised any of the people seated with Him in that synagogue. It would have been expected of any prospective Messiah. The people were expecting the Messiah to fulfill that role. Perrin's book makes clear that messianic expectation was closely connected with the end of exile themes and the recovery of Torah obedience on the matter of debt release. The people knew the Torah was being defied by the ruling class.

The people also knew from the prophet Jeremiah that the exile was due at least partially to disobedience to those rules. And they knew from the prophet Daniel that there was an interval of 490 years associating the Messiah with the end of exile and thus with the Sabbath year rules. Finally, it was well known that this 490-year period was about to come due.

Non-elite Israel was longing for a Messiah who would ensure debts were forgiven in accordance with the law and the prophets. Only then would they see the end of Israel's exile as a vassal of Rome. Jesus knew what He was doing by quoting these texts. He understood what the original context of these prophecies was and what the cultural and interpretive context was in which He preached their fulfillment. He quoted that passage without hedging it. If He didn't mean to make debt release an important part of His message, He would have invited misunderstanding.

If you are still in any doubt about whether Jesus meant debt forgiveness (not just spiritual sin forgiveness), then that doubt should be eliminated as you see how Jesus raised the debt issue in His first major large public speech, the Sermon on the Mount.

Jesus, Debt, and Prayer

Jesus's most famous public address is unquestionably what is known as "the Sermon on the Mount." In that discourse, He presents an example of a model prayer. This prayer includes the following:

> *And forgive us our debts, as we also have forgiven our debtors.*
>
> —Matthew 6:12

If you have read this far, you are well prepared to resist the habitual tendency of church tradition to spiritualize all the economics of this part of the prayer. Spiritualizing away the economic aspect of Jesus's statements about debt forgiveness amounts to ignoring the Old Testament teaching on debt. This hyperspiritual approach strains credulity. It requires us to believe that although the law and the prophets speak about debt forgiveness often, Jesus is ignoring all that teaching, despite being a Rabbi, and is starting a completely new conversation that focuses on debt. It also requires us to believe He did that in a sermon in which He explicitly reaffirms His commitment to the Old Testament Scriptures:

> *For truly I say to you, until heaven and earth pass away, not the smallest letter or stroke shall pass away from the Law, until all is accomplished.*
>
> *Whoever then annuls one of the least of these commandments, and so teaches others, shall be called least in the kingdom of heaven; but whoever keeps and teaches them, he shall be called great in the kingdom of heaven.*
>
> *For I say to you, that unless your righteousness surpasses that of the scribes and Pharisees, you shall not enter the kingdom of heaven.*
>
> —Matthew 5:18–20

And after that, are we to believe Jesus talks about debt forgiveness in a way that ignores the extensive debt forgiveness material found in the law and the prophets that we've reviewed above? Of course not.

Furthermore, Jesus's word choice in the debt forgiveness section of the Lord's Prayer is highly reminiscent of the language used regarding the Sabbath year debt provisions of the Septuagint, the Greek translation of the Old Testament, which was very commonly used during Jesus's time. The words emphasized below in English from Matthew 6, describing the debt release in the Lord's Prayer, run parallel to the words used in the debt forgiveness passage in Deuteronomy 15.

And forgive *us our* debts, *as also we* forgive *our* debtors.

—MATTHEW 6:12

...and this is the matter of the release: Every owner of a loan *is to release his hand which he doth lift up against his neighbour, he doth not exact of his neighbour and of his brother, but hath proclaimed a* release *to Jehovah.*

—DEUTERONOMY 15:2 (YLT) (emphases mine)

So the word that in Deuteronomy is typically translated as "release" in reference to debt is usually translated as "forgive" in the Lord's Prayer. But it's the same word. The most defensible interpretation is simply to say Jesus is doing exactly what He said He was going to do, affirming and fulfilling the law and the prophets, fulfilling the expected Messianic role that is to offer both debt release and forgiveness of sins.

Jesus knew Israel's ruling elites had ignored the law and the prophets and were well paid for doing so. This meant they were still flunking the test that caused Israel's captivity to foreign powers. Israel received a sort of partial relief, in that they were no longer captive to foreign empires outside their homeland. God graciously allowed Israel to return to their homeland, leaving them under almost uninterrupted "house arrest" for several centuries.

Rome was simply the most recent jailer overseeing their house arrest. Israel was exiled for failure to follow the sabbath laws, but when they returned from exile, they did not resume the sabbath laws.

Jesus tells this story in the thinly veiled Parable of the Ungrateful Servant. This parable explains that the lack of forgiveness is what will lead Israel into further, deeper judgment.

The Poor You Will Always Have with You, Aimed at the Ruling Class

We get so accustomed to reading the words of Jesus that they can become dead clichés. But when Jesus originally spoke, it was fresh, shocking, and new. We tend to interpret Jesus's words in light of tradition or our own personal religious sentiments. All those "Bible studies" in which the leaders read a passage and then ask the groups, "What does this mean to you?" have trained us to think our personal experience is the context through which to understand Jesus. But that's not what was going on in the First Century. Jesus was speaking in the context of the Old Testament and the conditions then in Israel.

That means they should be interpreted first in terms of the context in which they were given. That context first included the Old Testament, which was Jesus's and His disciples' Scriptures. That context also included historical circumstances extant at the time Jesus was speaking. He was, as He said, sent to the nation of Israel. He was sent to speak to "this generation," and that is what He did.

Let's use this basic, commonsense approach to look at one of those phrases that has become to many of us one of those dead clichés:

Now when Jesus was in Bethany, at the home of Simon the leper, a woman came to Him with an alabaster vial of very costly perfume, and she poured it upon His head as He reclined at the table.

But the disciples were indignant when they saw this, and said, "Why this waste?

"For this perfume might have been sold for a high price and the money given to the poor."

But Jesus, aware of this, said to them, "Why do you bother the woman? For she has done a good deed to Me.

"For the poor you have with you always; *but you do not always have Me.*"

—MATTHEW 26:6–11 (emphasis mine)

I don't think this is fortune cookie Jesus dispensing a pithy aphorism about the human condition. I think this is Rabbi Jesus, the Messiah of Israel, the incarnate Yahweh who is reiterating the warning He gave Israel a millennium and a half before, in Deuteronomy. Nicholas Perrin sees it too:

For when Jesus says, "You always have the poor with you," he is patently alluding to Deuteronomy, 15.1-11, a passage in which Moses enjoins the seventh year as the year of canceling (*shemittah*) debts.

The section of Deuteronomy is remarkable in its blend of idealism, realism, and pessimism. *"There will be* no one in need among you," so the text promises, "if only you will obey the LORD your God by diligently observing this entire commandment that I command you today" (vv. 4-5). But "*if* there is among you anyone in need," the scripture continues on a less confident note, "do not be hard-hearted or tight-fisted toward your needy neighbor" (v. 7).

This view is hardly unknown in the history of the church; Deuteronomy 15 is listed in the cross-references of at least one well-known Bible translation.

So why is it Israel would always have the poor with them? Because, as God warned them in Deuteronomy 15 (discussed above), they would not obey Him on the matter of debt remission. This may read as odd to modern Christians, who are not nearly as immersed in Old Testament texts as Jesus and His listeners were. Our interpretations tend to focus almost exclusively on heart issues and personal salvation (or for some, abstract theological formulations), whereas First Century Israel, although interested in heart attitudes, was consumed with outrage over the lack of debt relief and consumed with expectation about how the coming Messiah would proclaim liberty to the (debt) captives.

Jesus turned out to be right. Israel would not obey, and the poor would always be with them, right up until the end. In fact, the failure to obey God and the growing problem of debt and poverty would set in motion a series of events that would plunge the whole region into destruction.

Jesus's Debt Warnings, from Debt to Destruction

Sadly, it is often ignored by preachers that within a generation of Jesus's ministry Jerusalem was destroyed by Roman armies. Perhaps it is the tendency to treat everything in the Gospels as religious (meaning either about our personal salvation, our inner serenity, or the Second Coming) that causes us to ignore how very often Jesus did what He said He was sent to do: to call the house of Israel back to God, which includes obedience to quite a lot of God's commands about social and political matters, including economics.

Certainly, scholars are well aware of the destruction of Jerusalem looming over the Gospel accounts. In fact, liberal scholars have gone so far as to assert the Gospels are so clear in their allusions to this destruction they must have been written after the Fall of Jerusalem. That is, of course, nonsense. God knows the future and Jesus is God.

But even among those scholars who are aware of the Jerusalem destruction hanging over the Gospels, it is very much less well known that the chain of events leading to the destruction began with a reaction to excess debt. David Fiensy is the scholar who put me onto this theme:

> As is well known, Josephus does narrate one clear case of such an event in Palestine. In 66 CE during the Feast of Woodcarrying, the sicarii ("dagger carriers") and others broke forth into the upper city and set on fire the houses of Ananias the high priest and of Agippa I and Bernice. Then the mob turned to the public buildings:

After these things, they began to carry the fire to the archives [apxeta], being zealous to destroy the contracts of those who had loaned money and to cancel [aochopsai] the collection of debts. (*War* 2.427)

Josephus speculates at this point that the Sicarii hoped to win to their side a multitude [pleythos] of debtors.[19]

Debt had not yet reached full crisis level during Jesus's time on earth. (To learn more about this, see Fiensy's book.) However, by the time of AD 66, it appears debt levels had at last risen to crisis proportions, creating the preconditions to a debt revolt.

This revolt may have been triggered by the eventual completion of the temple and the end of the building boom associated with it. Construction on the temple complex, which had been going on for two full generations, had just been completed a year or two before the crisis began. The end of the project, of course, involved massive layoffs.

So, as we have seen so many times in history, a debt-fueled, public works project building boom ends in a bust. The uprising Josephus wrote about, which began with a debt revolt, came immediately after the end of this multigenerational Herodian building boom. The high priest's family was murdered. The debt records were burnt to the ground, but the crowd was not assuaged, and the violence spun out of control.

Eventually, Rome came to end it and ended up ending—not the violence—but the very city. Jesus's warnings were not heeded. Debt was compounded. The poor were always with them and were multiplied. Jesus warned the women of Jerusalem not to weep for Him but for their own children.

How bad was it? Very bad. Not only was the city of Jerusalem destroyed, but the waves of violence, then reactions to the violence, and then further violent reactions to violent reactions continued into the next generation. What little data we have shows the region did not recover for at least half a millennium. In some sense, it did not really recover its economic preeminence until now, two millennia later.

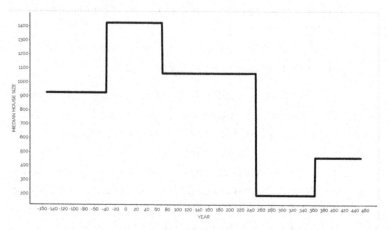

In the data above, you can see the economy booming before the destruction, then the destruction that drove home sizes (one of the best proxies for overall wealth) downward, then downward again with the Bar-Kochba rebellion (AD 132–136), where it stayed depressed for hundreds of years.

Jesus's message certainly included personal salvation, but it also included the possibility of national salvation as well, in the sense that He gave the nation of Israel the wisdom necessary to save itself from destruction. Jesus wept and longed to gather Jerusalem under His wings, to save them as a mother hen saves her chicks, but they would not.

CONCLUSION

What Does This Mean to Me?

I've done what I set out to do: to ask and to answer to the best of my ability, "What did Jesus's comments about wealth and poverty mean in historical context?" At the beginning of this book, I criticized the extremely common habit in modern Bible studies of starting with the question, "What does this verse mean to you?" I don't criticize this approach because I question the idea that we should apply the Bible to our own lives. I don't even criticize this approach to forbid people from using their own personal life experience as a tool in understanding the Bible. I criticize it because all too often we start with personal experience right away and stay there forever.

Instead, the approach I favor, as you have already seen, is to first go to what the text actually says. Not some vague, subjective "main point" of the text, but the actual word choices made, including details such as place names and occupations. Then we go to the historical context. The most important historical context for the New Testament is the Old Testament. After looking at the text carefully, not skimming over details, and viewing all that in light of the Old Testament, then we look at the historical context at the time Jesus was speaking. The context in Rome matters, but the context in ancient Israel matters even more. And, as you have already seen, the individual contexts of each of those provinces, cities, and villages in and around ancient Israel, in which Jesus spoke about matters of economics in different ways, matter a great deal as well.

But after we have done all that—after carefully reading the text in the original language, after a careful study of the Old Testament background, after consulting the history and archeology of First Century Israel—after all that is done, then we do need to ask, "What does this mean for us?"

We read it in context, trying to understand its intended meaning. Then we take that interpretation and apply it to our lives, with the understanding that we don't live in the same time and place and we have to think carefully as we translate the message from Jesus's context to our own. We build a bridge from the original context to now.

Let's look at a couple of examples. Jesus said, whoever looks at a woman to lust after her has already committed adultery with her in his heart. Okay, but what about pornography on the internet? There was no TV or internet when Jesus was speaking. People nowadays don't actually look at a woman to lust after her; they look at an image of a woman to lust after her. Yes, some people go to strip clubs, and so forth, but the internet is where people go to satisfy the lust of the eyes most often. Well, it seems pretty obvious to me that looking at web porn is pretty much the same thing. All the dangers associated with staring at an actual flesh and blood woman still seem to be present when staring at an electronic representation of one on a computer screen. Not too tough to build the bridge from then to now.

But what about Paul's admonition that women have their heads covered in church? Wherever you come down on this, it certainly seems like there's more translational work to do before we automatically apply that now. Why did Jesus tell men not to stare at women? Because it awakens a lust that is adulterous in nature. What about download porn? It's the same. It also awakens adulterous lusts. So, Jesus's prohibition there seems to translate over fairly directly. But why did Paul tell women to wear head coverings? Until you have some idea why he gave that order, it's hard to know how it applies to us.

Which brings us back to the topic of this book: Jesus's numerous statements about economic matters. Why did Jesus so often criticize state authorities, or those directly associated with state authorities, so directly and so often? Because they were corrupt and they used political power to take wealth from others. They were "robbers." The ruling class became self-serving, instead of serving the needs of the people. They became unfaithful stewards who tried to gain control of the vineyard for their own desire. They used power to extract wealth. They were not shepherds, nor even sheep. They were wolves in sheep's clothing, inwardly hungry for what did not belong to them.

Has that changed?

Does the principle still apply today? Well, you'll have to decide for yourself, but from what I've seen, it very much does. You might say our political class is different because in an age of democracy, government is forced to serve the good of the people, so our concentrations of political power are benign whereas the concentrations of power that Jesus confronted were malicious.

But as we saw in the story of Judas, the ruling elites of that place and time also claimed to be doing what they did for the good of the poor. That generation of rulers talked about sharing their wealth with the poor, but what they really did was force and/or manipulate the poor into sharing their wealth with the ruling class. That's the nature of power; it always claims to be serving the greater good, but it always arcs toward serving the great over the good.

Just as the fixed features of human nature we see in Jesus's warnings about lust apply two thousand years later, so the fixed features of the human lust for power also apply two thousand years later. It is dangerous for us to look at computer porn because we are still human. It is dangerous for us to entrust too much power to rulers because they are still human. Whether our babes and ballots are real life or paper or digital does not really change the nature of either. Libido and *libido dominandi* ("the lust for power" per Saint Augustine) are part of human nature as much now as they were then.

This means that any follower of Jesus who wants to assert any ideology that requires concentrations of power in the state must first show us why those who operate the levers of power in our time will do it less selfishly than those who pulled those levers in Jesus's time.

After all, this was Israel, the most Biblical nation on earth. It had the Temple of God. It had the very oracles of God, the Scriptures. No nation on earth had as much truth as ancient Israel. Yet even they blew it. Little by little, the lure of wealth and power corrupted that society, especially the political elites. Why does anyone think we would be immune to this?

We're different? Why? How? Show me.

Now, it might seem like I'm being partisan about this because the Republicans like to talk about shrinking the state and decentralizing power. Well, maybe they used to like to talk that way. But that was before. Both parties look like big state parties to me now. And if you look at actions, not rhetoric, perhaps Republicans have been a big state party longer than many of us have been willing to admit.

Now both parties are aflame with the rhetoric of populism. Donald Trump was elected to "drain the swamp." His Democrat critics say he can't drain the swamp because he *is* the swamp. According to the Bible, we *all* are the swamp, dust, and brackish water. History will show this generation what it has shown every generation before—we all bring the swamp with us when we come into power. No group is virtuous enough or smart enough or great enough or has enough common sense or money or diplomas or four-dimensional chess skills to wield vast power over others and not turn whatever capitol they rule from into swamp land.

The difference between Galilee and Judea was not that the people of Galilee were inherently better people. They were of the same stock. The difference is the Galileans did not have much access to the levers of power. Most of them ate bread by the sweat of their brow, because they had no alternative. It's the same for us. Once power and status are concentrated someplace, the people there immediately begin to turn into Judeans, Romans, Washingtonians, the "ruling class," the establishment, the "deep state."

Conclusion

Maybe that's one of the reasons God allowed His temple to be torn down and then rebuilt "wherever two or three are gathered together in My Name": because the central sanctuary in the central city under a human central king became exactly what God warned Israel in the law and the prophets it would be: a source of temptation and tyranny. Of course, we messed that up, too.

Jesus denounced the ruling power factions in His time, the Herodians and the Sadducees. But He also denounced competing power blocks as well, such as the Pharisees. He even criticized His own Galileans harshly enough that they tried to kill Him. If Jesus merely had a problem with the people who happened to be in charge, then why did He not back one of the many opposition groups? Because none was righteous, no, not one. No mere human was, and therefore no mere human could be entrusted with power.

Only living water can drain the swamp, the living water that comes from Christ alone. Only One could bear the crown and not become part of the swamp, and His was a crown of thorns, which no one but He was willing to bear on His brow.

And that is as true now as it was then.

Christians should be the last people to sign up for massive concentrations of economic power in the state. And when it is done in the name of the poor, we should remember Judas.

We can either have a big state and a small god or we can have a big God and a small state.

Put not your trust in princes, nor in the son of man, in whom there is no help.

His breath goeth forth, he returneth to his earth; in that very day his thoughts perish.

Happy is he that hath the God of Jacob for his help, whose hope is in the LORD his God.

—Psalm 146:3–5 (KJV)

Endnotes

1. Alfred Edersheim, *The Life and Times of Jesus the Messiah* (Peabody, Massachusetts: Hendrickson Publishers, 1993), 186–87.

2. *Omaha World-Herald*, "Daniel L. Dreisbach: The Declaration, the Constitution, the Bible," accessed March 9, 2020, https://www.omaha.com/opinion/daniel-l-dreisbach -the-declaration-the-constitution-the-bible/article_8d5b4cb0-6030-11e7-b329 -df0efc8f97e4.html.

3. Nicholas Perrin, *Jesus the Temple* (Ada, Michigan: Baker Academic, 2010), 123.

4. John Wesley, Wesley's Explanatory Notes—Luke 10, BibleStudyTools.com, accessed March 23, 2020, https://www.biblestudytools.com/commentaries/wesleys-explan-atory-notes/luke/luke-10.html.

5. David Fiensy, *Christian Origins and the Ancient Economy* (Eugene, Oregon: Cascade Books, 2018).

6. Franklin D. Roosevelt, "First Inaugural Address," Saturday, March 4, 1933, Bartleby. com, accessed March 10, 2020, https://www.bartleby.com/124/pres49.html.

7. Alfred Edersheim, *The Temple: Its Ministry and Services, as They Were at the Time of Jesus Christ* (Franklin Classics, 2017).

8. Flavius Josephus, *The Complete Works of Flavius Josephus* (JOE), trans. William Whiston (Auburn and Buffalo, NY: John E. Beardsley, 1895), BibleWorks, vol. 10.

9. C. D. Yonge, *The Works of Philo* (Peabody, Massachusetts: Hendrickson Publishers, 1991).

10. Josephus.

11. Otto Lightner, *A History of Business Depressions* (Franklin Classics, 2018), 20–21.

12. Ibid.

13. William L. Holladay, *A Concise Hebrew and Aramaic Lexicon of the Old Testament* (Grand Rapids, Michigan: William B. Eerdmans Publishing Company, 1972).

14. Francis Brown, S. R. Driver, and Charles A. Briggs, *Brown-Driver-Briggs Hebrew and English Lexicon* (California: Snowball Publishing, 2011).

15. Ibid.

16 Ibid, 191–192. Edersheim.
17 Ibid. Perrin.
18 Ibid, 62. Fiensy.
19 Ibid, 65, Fiensy.

ACKNOWLEDGMENTS

I've noticed that all too often, acknowledgments sections of books have a higher proportion of people who might help the author in the future than have already helped the author in the creation of the book in hand. I will try to avoid using this as a networking-upward tool.

First, there is Susan Bowyer. There's no page in this book that wasn't a conversation with her long before becoming part of a book. She's not just the inspiration for everything I write, she's a co-thinker for all of it as well.

A lot of this started thirty-six years ago when I listened to James Jordan's lectures on Matthew 24, and it dawned on me that perhaps I should rethink my factory-installed evangelical default setting that treats almost everything Jesus said as being about either the afterlife or the second coming. I don't even remember exactly what Jordan specifically said about that discourse, how much is near future vs. far future, only that a new option opened for me—a Jesus who commented on the matters of His time and place. James Jordan is now at Theopolis Institute, whose chairman, Reverend Jeff Meyers, and whose president, Dr. Peter Leithart, have been good conversation partners about these ideas.

The next big step was a meeting with Ed Atsinger, CEO of Salem (okay, I only said I'd try not to network upwards), who said to me, "Read N. T. Wright. I think you're going to like him." And so, I did read him, and so I did like him—mostly. Sometimes he ticked me off, but some of those times he eventually changed my mind. Wright helped me understand with greater detail how historical context could help us see dimensions of the Gospel texts that a strictly "theological" or "eschatological" reading tended to ignore. Every few years, I'd have a chat with Dr. Wright on the radio, or via podcast and occasional correspondence, as I filled out that understanding and, I hope and pray, built on the foundation he had laid by adding the knowledge of a practicing economist to historical analysis.

My friend and pastoral mentor, Reverend Canon Doctor Father Jay Geisler, is the first person to talk to me about Sepphoris, after which I learned as much as I possibly could. Then he generously opened his own pulpit to let me actually preach about such things.

Paul Maier's book *Pontius Pilate: A Novel* (as well as some of his nonfiction work) helped me connect the crucifixion with the Sejanus crisis in Rome, and once we had that in place, the role of the financial crisis flowed out of that.

Alfred Edersheim, too-much neglected in our age, was very helpful at points, especially in *The Temple: Its Ministry and Services.*

Speaking of the temple, Nicholas Perrin's *Jesus the Temple* was also very helpful in getting me up to speed regarding what we've learned since Edersheim's day.

David Fiensy's book *Christian Origins and the Ancient Economy* opened my eyes to the flood of economic archeology coming out of Galilee. His two-volume work with James Riley Strange, *Galilee in the Late Second Temple and Mishnaic Periods,* was a treasure trove of detail about the economy in which Jesus grew up.

Sharp eyes may well discern the influence of René Girard on my analysis. His disciple Peter Thiel has been a helpful sounding board for some of the points regarding Jesus's reasons for using parables to obscure his message, and his encouragement on this point also helped me decide this really does deserve a book-length treatment.

I also thank my friends at Kingdom Advisors, Ron Blue and Rob West, for letting me share these ideas as they have developed over several years. When Rob called me after reading the feedback forms from conference goers and told me, "It looks like you're really onto something," that also helped move me into the "yes" column when it came to turning this research into a book. Then again, maybe I misheard him—maybe he actually said, "You're really on something." Time will tell.

Thank you also to my friend and colleague Vince Birley, CEO of Vident Financial, and his predecessor there, Nick Stonestreet, who never once pressured me to use valuable presentation time in front of a room full of successful financial advisors, potential clients every one, to push our business services. "Educate, don't sell" is not financial industry standard.

I'm thankful for the invitation to present these ideas at Oxford University's Wycliffe Hall from Rick Goossen of the Entrepreneurial Leadership Programme, and for his encouragement and that of Justyn Terry, vice principal, Wycliffe Hall. This was another cup of water along the marathon race that encouraged me to press on.

Then there is my brother and Samurai, Gary Terashita, who repeatedly talked me out of talking myself out of writing this book. He's that best of experts, an expert with skin in the game.

I apologize to anyone who contributed to this book but whom I did not acknowledge. But I do have it on good authority that He who sees in secret will reward openly.